GODS, HEROES AND MYTHS

The most beautiful stories of Greek Mythology

Title: GODS, HEROES AND MYTHS

The most beautiful stories of Greek Mythology

Author: Anna Morena Mozzillo

Grafic Design: Pierluigi Pastore

To the Eternal Children

*And to Mark Gaydos, friend and engineer,
who reviewed the English text.*

...Then one of the priests, a very old man said: "Solon, Solon, you Greeks are always children, and there is not an old Greek"...

"There is in Egypt", he began, "in the Delta, at whose apex the Nile divides, a district called Saite, and Sais is the most important city of this district; the city came from the king Amasis. For residents a goddess was the founder of the town, and her name in Egyptian is Neith; while in Greek, they say Athena; they are very good friends of the Athenians, and in a sense, they say they are still their relatives. Solon said that, coming to that place, he was welcomed with great honor among them, and that having once asked about the Ancient facts, the priests prepared more aroun these issues. He found that neither he nor any other Greek was, as it were, aware of these circumstances. And then wanting to push them to talk about ancient events he began to talk about those facts that he believed to be the oldest. He told of Phoroneus, said to be the first man, and Niobe, and after the flood, how Deucalion and Pyrrha spent their lives, and produced their descendants. Remembering the times he tried to calculate in which years the events he spoke of had occurred.

Then one of the priests, a very old man said: "Solon, Solon, you Greeks are always children, and there is not an old Greek". And Solon, after listening, asked, "What? What is this thing you say?" "You are all young people," said the priest, "in spirit. In fact you have no ancient opinion that comes from a primitive tradition, nor any teaching that is gray with age. And this is the reason. There are many ways, and there have been many, and there shall be the loss of men; the greatest by fire and water and for many other lesser reasons.

That story is told that with you, that is to say that one day Phaethon, son of the Sun, having yoked his father's chariot, and since he was incapable of driving it along the path of his father, burned everything that was on the ground, and he himself was killed struck by lightning. It is told in the form of myth, but actually it is the deviation of the celestial bodies that revolve around the earth, and determines long destruction intervals by fire, all that is on earth."

Plato, TIMAEUS

INDEX

THE OLYMPIANS

The Twelve Olympian Gods

Zeus

Hera

Poseidon

Hermes

Aphrodite

Ares

Hestia

Phoebus

Artemis

Hephaestus

Demeter

Athena

Dionysus

OTHER GODS AND LEGENDS

Pan

Asclepius

Helios and the Chariot of the Sun

The Dioscuri Castor and Pollux

Aeolus, the God of the Winds

The Nine Muses

Prometheus and the Gift of Fire

Pandora

Deucalion and Pyrrha

Cadmus and the Dragon's Teeth

Daedalus and Icarus

Theseus and the Minotaur

Orpheus and Eurydice

Perseus and Medusa

Bellerophon and the Chimaera

Tantalus

Pelops and Hippodamia

Introduction

Myth

The word "myth" in Greek originally meant "word" or "speech". Then, it meant "story"- primarily the story of facts determined by superior forces, deities and supernatural beings involved in the human sphere. It is very difficult to determine how and why myths were born. We can only imagine the scenarios that were presented to men after upheavals, cataclysms, floods, sinking of the lands and the emergence of others, volcanic eruptions; a hostile and inhospitable world beaten by rain and wind, struck by lightning, storms, earthquakes, floods, etc.

In this world, man had to live with wild animals, often gigantic, from which he had to defend himself. He had to learn to survive in adverse conditions; he learned to know the alternation of day and night. He learned to use fire for his needs, to build shelters and weapons. In short, he began the process of civilization. But all that the man saw was not subjected to his rule; all that was not foreseeable, or that it wasn't manageable with his abilities. He imagined it was the work of supernatural beings, the immense power that could be beneficial or destructive. Stories were formed about hidden or unknown beings, who operated from the depths of the earth, from the heights of the sky, or from the depths of the sea. Stories and legends were told that little by little became more complex, that intertwined with each other, that were also changed over time or in different places.

They envisioned creatures that were not very different from men, but with extraordinary powers who held the fate of the world and of human beings. By changing the circumstances and the events as they pleased, they had to be so benevolent through sacrifices and rituals, in which they had to bring offerings to ensure that they became propitious

It's likely at the beginning, as still happens to primitive civilizations, each tribe has created its tutelary deity, i.e., a totem, which is an animal, a plant or an object worshiped for its supernatural virtues, that became the symbol of each tribe and its unifying element. Man then got in touch with the world of the divine and began building a dense network of stories and legends, myths, trying to explain the events of creation

With all ancient peoples there are collections of legends that attempt to create a certain vision of the world, that tell of the origins of the universe, of the appearance of the first gods, or of the many other deities that were gradually generated or created by an indistinct space. At first these stories were passed down orally, because writing was not yet known; among all peoples in fact initially we find the oral transmission of the heritage of fabulous stories, formed and expanded over the centuries. Only later, when the use of writing appeared, were these legends fixed in written texts and began to spread.

For a long time, for centuries, all these stories circulated only through oral transmission, that is, the story was transmitted by singers to listeners. In ancient Greece in particular, a large number of legends developed, that spoke of the beginning of a chaotic and messy world, that little by little, with the help of many deities, became civilized and tidy. These stories became part of the repertoire of many artists, poets, painters and sculptors, who took inspiration from the myths and reworked them, or they created others. Each singer (in Greece called "bard"), probably repeated what he had learned from others. He may have added something of his own, sometimes even changing some details of the story; it happened so often that the same myth exists in different versions, with different episodes or details that are partially or completely different. For example, in the Pelasgian myth the divine couple from which creation originates is composed of Eurynome and Ophion; however, as we shall see, the poet Homer has humanity descending from Oceanus and Tethys.

The ancient Greeks had other versions of the origin of the world. As we will see later, we find in Hesiod the primordial couple Uranus and Gaea; in Ovid we will see that there is a lord god of all things, etc. In fact the narrator was often not particularly interested that what he told was based on documented facts. The important thing was to hand to hand down to posterity the legends formed over time. They were not only entertainment or poems, but expressed in the guise of fairy tales and moral teachings, the social and religious values of a given society.

Mythology

The term means "the study of myths." We have already said what myths are. These are stories, passed down orally from the beginning, from generation to generation, from father to son, telling of gods and heroes, fantastic creatures and monsters. The imagination of the ancient Greeks left us a rich heritage of legends that have fascinated people over the centuries, and still fascinate readers of all ages. Artists of all time drew on mythological stories to write, paint, sculpt their works. The fate that met and meets mythology should perhaps be explained by the need that man has to sometimes overcome reality in order to raise himself in the world of fantasy, of dreams. But we should not believe that everything we find in the legends is the work of imagination; very often the myths reflect a primitive's attempt to explain to himself the universe in which he lives, one that seems mysterious and often threatening. The origin of myth must therefore be sought in man's need to understand the elements of nature that surround him, giving an explanation, albeit fantastic, to what he sees happening around him.

Mythology is not then a dry series of events in a distant time, but a wealth of stories about man and his history, expressing ideas that are always valid and profoundly human. Through it people kept the memory of their origins, showed the memories and values of the community to which they belonged, and expressed their religious beliefs. Mythology collects narratives concerning fantastic events that took place in ancient times. Protagonist gods, heroes and demi-gods, strange and monstrous creatures, and even men, are used to explain the various natural phenomena which man attends, or origin of the universe, or the origin of man himself, or the birth of the major institutions of society.

Often mythology is "sacred narrative". It has a religious meaning, and refers to the moral values of a community or of an entire people. These narratives are called "epics", a term derived from the word "epos", which means "word" or "verse". The epic songs, as we said, were mostly anonymous in ancient time, that is, not attributable to a specific person. Most often they were the work of different singers who had the task of passing on with their verses the values of their time and their society, the memory of the history of the people to which they belonged. For us modern readers myths have essentially narrative character. They are stories that belong to a literary genre, the epic. It is a kind of poetry that deals with a given topic; it has an evolution, sometimes cruel, sometimes auspicious or even funny. It presents characters who perform actions, according to a certain story.

Even today these myths capture our attention. We enjoy them; they form the basis of many works of art produced by contemporaries.

Science today has explained many things and always progresses to explain others; but questions and doubts still remain on many aspects of our lives. We can even say that the more one knows about the world around us, the more one realizes how much still remains to be discovered. It is important to continue to investigate nature and the world around us. Man probably will never cease to do so, but it is also important sometimes to indulge the imagination and go back to the origins of the world, to the stories of the ancient men, sometimes naive, sometimes fanciful or unreal, but which retain all their charm over time.

THE ORIGINS

Cosmogony

One of the topics that have aroused most interest among ancient peoples and which still fascinates modern man, is related to the origin of the world. Mythology speaks about it, with a term derived from the greek, the "Cosmogonia", the "origin of the universe". Every ancient people tried to give its answers to the question of how the universe was formed. Egyptians, Babylonians, Indians, etc., have formulated their theories, their "creation myths".

Also in Greece, they considered this aspect so important that many myths were developed. These were all very impressive and the most famous are the Pelasgian creation myth and the Olympic myth. Pelasgic is derived from the Pelasgians, who were the ancient inhabitants of Greece before the arrival of Indo-Europeans. These people colonized much of Central and Southern Asia and Europe in successive waves. The Indo-Europeans are so called because they gave rise to European and Indian civilization, and are the progenitors of many people, the most important of which are: Slavs, Germans, Celts, Italians (and Latins), Phrygians, Greeks, Illyrians, Anatolian, Iranians, Indians and Armenians.

Studies to better understand the migration and the spread of these peoples have sprung from their languages, and we have seen that they have a common origin, found in Proto Indo-European, the ancient language of the Indo-European or Aryans, as they were also called. It's interesting to note that similar myths and legends are found in places and peoples very distant from each other, most likely because they are derived from a common source. These myths of origins are characterized by strange and sometimes confused stories. We feel in them the echo of big changes on the earth's surface, when the mixture of primitive elements began to shape the look of the world as we see it today. So there are storms and blizzards, floods, earthquakes and volcanic eruptions, creation and destruction of land, islands and mountains. The Latin poet Ovid says in his book "The Metamorphosis": "Before the sea, before the earth and the sky that covers everything, uniform was the look of nature; and they called it Chaos."

Chaos is a Greek word that means "disorder, confused state of the elements." From this chaotic universe, we proceed to an ordered universe: the Cosmos. Cosmos in the Greek language means "order." In archaic myths the birth of the universe is connected to the birth of the gods, which is called by the Greek word "Theogony".

The legends recall the events of three successive kingdoms. We always see at the head a god leading a host of other lesser gods; so we remember the first reign of Uranus (Heaven), a second reign of Cronos (Time) and a third kingdom, one that was to remain permanently, that of Zeus (Jupiter in Latin). Each of these three kingdoms breaks down the previous through violence and deception. These legends seem to say that to achieve balance we too must face troubled times.

It's very likely that in these myths there are also distant memories of the power struggles that really existed on Earth; do not forget that in ancient times war was unfortunately a widespread phenomenon.

Analysis and Understanding

1) What does the term "cosmology" mean? From what language is it derived?
2) Which ancient peoples formulated theories on the origin of the universe, besides the Greeks?
3) What is a "creation myth"?
4) What is the derivation of the term "Pelasgian"?
5) Why are Indo-European peoples so called? By what other name they are called?
6) Which are the most important Indo-European peoples?
7) There are studies on the common origin of these peoples and their migrations; what observations started research into this topic?
8) What is the name of the ancient language of the Indo-Europeans?
9) What does the term "Theogony" mean?
According to the legend which were the first three successive kingdoms?

Reworking and Writing

1) Do a quick search on the Indo-European peoples.

2) How does modern science explain the origin of the Universe? Have you ever heard of the Big Bang? Find news about it.

Eurynome and Ophion

In the Pelasgic myth of the origins of the world it is said that Eurynome (which means "one who wanders, or controls, in ample space") was born from Chaos (not Disorder, as we will later understand the term, but "empty space"). She began to dance in this immense space, and dancing faster and faster with her movements, gave birth to the wind Boreas. This became the snake Ophion; transformations, or metamorphosies, as they are also called, appear frequently in the Greek myths. Afterwards Eurynome, transformed into a dove, deposited the cosmic egg; around this egg Ophion, by order of the goddess, coiled itself seven times to protect it. From the cosmic egg were born all things: the sun, the moon, the stars, the planets, the earth, the mountains, the rivers, the trees and living creatures. Eurynome and Ophion then settled on Mount Olympus, but at some point they began to quarrel, because Ophion began to boast of having created all things. So Eurynome, angry, kicked him and knocked out all of his teeth (from these were born the first men) and forced him into underground caverns. We should not be surprised by this violence; it will be a common feature in several mythological stories. Do not forget that these stories were created in a primitive time, not yet fully civilized, when violence was unfortunately widespread. But back to Eurynome, the goddess thus remained the only sovereign of creation; she created the seven planetary powers (Sun, Moon, Mars, Mercury, Jupiter, Venus, Saturn), and at the head of each of them she put a Titan and a Titaness, gigantic and powerful creatures.

Legend says that the first men were born from the teeth of Ophion. The first of them would be called Pelasgus and would be born from the land of Arcadia. Later the other men would be born, and Pelasgus would teach them to build shelters, to dress with animal skins, to get food, etc. In other words, he would give them the first signs of civilization. Legend has it that Eurynome and Ophion then rushed into the waters of Oceanus, and their power passed to Cronos and Rhea.

The myths don't always explain why the events happen. In this case we think that through the succession of different deities in power, they wanted to symbolize the difficult path of man towards a peaceful and civil order. In several of these creation myths the element water has great importance, and this is understandable when you consider how important is water for human life on planet Earth, even today. Indeed, it is not only important, but essential to life; we could not live without water. Therefore it's normal that our ancestors gave water a predominant role in the creation of the world. At that time science had not advanced as far as it has today, so they did not even know that the Earth was spherical. We must look to the Pythagoreans philosophers, Pythagoras and his followers (sixth century B. C. until the third century) to find the first theory of the sphericity of the Earth. So in the ancient accounts of creation it is easy to find the vision of a flat world, where there is "above" and "below", a division between Heaven and Earth, that originates from a division of the elements first mixed in the original Chaos.

Analysis and Understanding

1) What does the name "Eurynome" mean?
2) Where she was born?
3) What is meant by Chaos in this myth?
4) What was Ophion called before his transformation into a snake?
5) Why did Eurynome and Ophion quarrel?
6) What did Ophion do?
7) What was born from the teeth of Ophion?
8) According to this legend, what was the name of the first man?
9) What did Pelasgus teach the first humans?

10) Who came to power after the fall of Eurynome and Ophion into the Oceanus?

Reworking and Writing

1) Put into the text a dialogue describing the quarrel between Eurynome and Ophion.

2) The study of prehistory, the first period of history when there are no written records, teaches us the different names by which the first men in the long path of evolution are known. Do a little research on the subject.

The Creation Myth in Homer - The Great Mother

The Pelasgian myth we have just read is similar to the myth of the birth of the world that we find in Homer. He tells of creation taking place by the merging of Oceanus, the river that flowed around the whole world, and Thetys, the mother of all things. Indeed Eurynome is another aspect of the myth of the Great Mother, the great Goddess Earth, creator of all things, that is present in many ancient mythologies. It could also be the deity of matriarchal societies, i. e., societies in which women have greater powers; most likely this kind of society existed at the beginning, before it was supplanted by patriarchal society, in which the oldest male of the family group is in charge.

In many mythologies, in fact, among the various ancient peoples, there is an ancient female deity, the Great Mother, symbol of earth, fertility, who is a mediator between the human and the divine world. Some think that her cult is connected to a phase of human history in which matriarchal societies prevailed, one during which there were hunter-gatherers.

It's certain that the worship of female deities was present during the Neolithic period, and probably also in the Paleolithic, because all over Europe figurines depicting female figures, the so-called "Venus", have been found. With the passage of time the diverse cultures became increasingly complex. The cult of the Great Mother is divided into many minor aspects with many attributions to particular deities; thus the goddesses who oversaw love developed: Ishtar in Mesopotamia, Astarte in Phoenician-Palestine, Cybele in Anatolian, Aphrodite in Greece and Venus in Romae. There were also those who were the guardians of fertility of women, Hecate; those that protected the fertility of the fields, Demeter, Persephone or Proserpina and those who presided over the hunt, Artemis, and Diana.

Often the cult of the Great Goddess was linked to the cycle of death and rebirth, as well as to nature that seems to fall asleep or be reborn with the seasons, or the seed that seems to die to produce new life. A close relationship existed between the cycle of life and the cycle of the moon. Repetitions are even found in the symbols used to depict these goddesses and show the common origin of such veneration. Often these goddesses have dominion over animals, for example the snake, which is a chthonic symbol, i.e., of the earth. Very often their domains are forests, caves and springs; thus the nocturnal nature of cults is very strong.

Analysis and Understanding

1) According to Homer, how did creation take place?
2) Eurynome is an aspect of which other god?
3) What is a patriarchal society? And a matriarchal society?
4) What is the symbol of the Great Mother?
5) What are the so-called "Venuses"?
6) Who are the goddesses who oversaw love among the various ancient peoples?
7) Who are the goddesses who protected the fertility of the fields?
8) Why is the cult of the Great Mother linked to the cycle of death and rebirth?
9) Why do we find the repetition of symbols representing these different female deities?
10) What does "chthonic" mean?

Reworking and Writing

1) Do a search on matriarchal societies.

2) In the mythical tales about creation, are space and time well defined? Reply explaining why.

The Olympian Creation Myth

The myths that tell of the origin of the world are quite confused and vague. They are populated by a number of more or less important gods, each with its own characteristics. The Olympian creation myth tells that from Chaos, the indistinct void, Mother Earth, Gaea, emerged and gave birth to Uranus (Heaven). He sent rain upon the earth, so that grass, trees, flowers, wild animals and birds arose. From the rains, the rivers were also generated, and the lakes and seas formed.

Gaea then bore three children with an almost human aspect, the giants with a hundred arms called Centimani or, using a term derived from the Greek, Hecatonchires. These were Briareus (strong), Gyges (born from the earth) and Cotto (progenitor of the Cotti, the people of Thrace, a region of Greece).

Then Gaea begot three Cyclopes, giants with only one eye, builders of walls and expert blacksmiths:

Bronte (Thunder), Sterope (Lightning) and Arge (bright).

The Odyssey, Homer's famous poem, tells that Ulysses encountered their descendants in Sicily, during his wanderings on the return to his homeland, the island of Ithaca. In the famous episode Homer tells how Ulysses, after getting the Cyclops Polyphemus drunk, blinded him with a sharpened stake and then fled with his companions, hidden under the sheep that Polyphemus brought out from the cave the next morning. But back to the creation of the world as the "Olympic" myth tells us.   According to legend, the mother Earth then generates these strange, gigantic beings.   Perhaps they represent the unpredictable and uncontrollable forces of nature.

It's likely, as some say, that the Cyclopes, a term that means "round eyes", are nothing but volcanic craters, throwing stones and burning embers just as those monsters in the mythical representations do, as Polyphemus does in vain against Ulysses, while he moves away on his ship, by now rescued.

Regarding the term Uranus, it took the meaning of "Heaven", but for some students it would be the masculine form of Urana, that is, the queen of the mountains, of the summer, of the winds, a goddess of the peak of summer.

It is also likely, according to other historians of antiquity, that the marriage of Uranus with mother

Earth, recalls the invasion of the Hellenes (Greeks) in the Greek peninsula, where they worshiped the Mother Goddess.

Some ancient authors spoke of terrible clashes between Heaven and Earth, which were then reunited by love.

Someone wanted to see in this, a fight and then a reunion between different peoples.

They believed that there was a merger, after the first shock, between the two different social groups, and between the two different societies, the patriarchal one of the Hellenes and the matriarchal one of the indigenous people.

Analysis and Understanding

1) Who were the Centimani and what were their names?
2) How were the Cyclopes generated by Gaea and what were their names?
3) Which famous Homeric hero had to do with the Cyclops Polyphemus?
4) What would the strange and monstrous beings generated from the Earth mean to some?
5) What does "Cyclops"mean?
6) What does "indigenous" people mean?
7) What people invaded the Greek peninsula?
8) What do historians of antiquity think of this marriage between Heaven and Earth?
9) What does the name "Uranus"mean?
10) Who were the Greeks?

Reworking and Writing

1) Research and briefly describe the episode of Odysseus and the Cyclops Polyphemus, as we read in Homer's Odyssey.

2) Do a search on the so-called "Dorian invasion" in the Greek peninsula.

The Titanomachia

This strange word, like many others we have already found, comes from the Greek and means "the struggle of the Titans." The Titans were strong mythological beings, six sons and six daughters of Uranus and Gaea, Heaven and Earth, the overlords of the universe, for long ages.

Uranus, the sky, had expelled his children, the Cyclopes, to Tartarus, because they had dared to rebel. Tartarus was the dark underground world, as far from the earth as the earth was far from heaven.

Then Gaea, Mother Earth, convinced other children, the Titans, to move against their father; the bravest was Cronos, the youngest. He wounded Uranus, so that he fled and retreated from the Earth, never to return. Then the Titans freed the Cyclopes from Tartarus and entrusted command to Cronos. However, once Cronos had the power, doubting their loyalty, he imprisoned his brother

Titans, as well as the Cyclopes and the Centimani, in Tartarus. He had them guarded by Campe, who was a female monster.

Then Cronos married Rhea and began to rule, but there was a prophecy, according to which, one of the sons of Cronos, when he grew up, would take power from his father. So every year Cronos devoured his children by Rhea: first Hestia, then Demeter and Hera, Hades and finally, Poseidon.

Their mother Rhea, angry, when she had the last-born, Zeus, in order to save him, turned him over to Cronos's mother, Gaea, the Earth. She took him to the island of Crete and hid him in a cave, guarded by the Nymphs and nurtured by the goat Amalthea.

The cradle of Zeus was hung from the branches of a tree, so that it could not be found in heaven, on earth nor in the sea. Thus Cronos could not find him. In front of the cave two soldiers, the Curetes, stood guard. They muffled the cries of the baby Zeus by forcefully beating their swords on their shields and shouting war hymns, so the cries of the child could not be heard.

Meanwhile Rhea had swaddled a rock and brought it to Cronos, making him believe that it was the baby. He swallowed it, thinking that he had also eliminated his youngest son. Instead, Zeus grew up among the shepherds of Mount Ida. He became great and managed, with the help of his mother Rhea, to have the post of cupbearer of Cronos, to be able to carry out a plan. His mother gave him an emetic potion, which he had his father drink. So Cronos vomited the stone, and both the brothers and the sisters of Zeus, whom he had eaten earlier. The stone was taken instead by Zeus to Delphi, Greece, and became the center of the world, "the navel of the world", as it was called.

Grateful to Zeus, his brother and sister gods decided to help him battle the Titans who had been freed from Cronos and who had not accepted the new dominion of Zeus; they chose the giant Atlas as their leader.

The war between the gods and the Titans lasted ten years. A prophecy had foretold that the gods would win if they allied with those whom Cronos had exiled to Tartarus.

Zeus then freed the Cyclopes and the Centimani, reanimating them with the divine nectar. The Cyclopes gave to Zeus the thunderbolt, to Hades a helmet of invisibility and to Poseidon a trident, so the three prevailed over Cronos and the Titans. In fact, they were driven off by a hail of stones hurled by the Centimani and were terrified by a scream of the god Pan, who scared away them.

The losers ended up exiled in the far west, under the guard of the Giants with one hundred arms. Their leader Atlas was punished even more harshly; exiled to the end of the world, he was sentenced to carry forever the weight of the heavens on his shoulders. Some say, however, that the old Cronos was given special treatment: he was exiled to the Elysian Fields, the kingdom of the Underworld, and became its king. The female Titans were spared because they had not taken part in the struggle. Also Oceanus was kept in the background, along with his wife Tethys, remaining in his watery world.

The struggle between the Titans and the gods symbolizes the struggle between the dark forces of Chaos, disorder primordial, and the divine order, the law that needed to be imposed on the universe, the cosmos. After the war and their subsequent victory, three gods divided power in a draw. It established that Hades was given the underground kingdom, which was also called Hades, of course; Poseidon received the marine realm and Zeus would rule the universe.

Analysis and Understanding

1) What was Tartarus, and whom did Uranus imprison there?
2) Who Cronos was, and what did he do?
3) Who married Cronos?
4) Why did Cronos devour his children when he came to power?
5) How did Rhea managed to save Zeus from his father?
6) Who fed the baby Zeus?

7) Who was the leader of the Titans?
8) How was he punished after he was defeated?
9) What did the Cyclopes presented to the three gods Zeus, Poseidon and Hades?
10) Where Cronos was exiled?

Reworking and Writing

1) Cronos in Greek means "time". In your opinion, what is the significance of the fact that he devoured his own children?
2) Explain how this myth tries to express the importance of the transition from an initial chaotic state to the birth of civilization.

The Gigantomachia

Gaea, Mother Earth, wife of Uranus, was unforgiving to Zeus because of his victory over the Titans, her children, and their imprisonment in Tartarus, so she instigated her other children, the Giants, to move against the Olympians. They were huge, powerful creatures, with shaggy hair and bristly beards. Their names were Typhon, Enceladus, Agrio, Thoas, Ephialtes, Eurytus, Pallas, and others. Their leaders were Alcyoneus and Porphyry. Alcyoneus, in particular, was outstanding among all others in stature and strength.

The fight was long and hard and took place in several regions, from Sicily to the Campi Flegrei in Campania, from Arcadia to Thessaly, from Macedonia to Thrace. To reach the summit of Mount Olympus, the home of the gods, it is said that the Giants even placed one mountain on top of another. A prophecy foretold, however, that no immortal god could overcome the Giants, if at least one mortal man did not intervene as an ally of the gods. Zeus, knowing this, had his son Heracles partecipate in the struggle, since he was mortal, having been born of a mortal, Alcmene.

A furious battle began: Alcyoneus, the leader of the Giants, was struck by a dart from Heracles, but could not die in the land of his birth, for he was protected from this. So Athena took him away, since only in this way could he be defeated. Zeus struck Porphyry with lightning. He was then killed with an arrow of Hercules; Apollo struck Ephialtes; Dionysus killed Eurytus; Athena threw the entire island of Sicily onto Enceladus, imprisoning him under it. Poseidon struck Polybotes with a piece of the island of Kos, which he broke with his trident, and that became the rock of Nisiro. Hermes killed Ippolito; Artemis pierced Gratione; while Zeus stunned all the Giants with lightning, and Heracles struck them with his arrows. So finally this fight also ended, and Zeus was able to reign undisturbed over the entire universe with the other Olympic gods.

It should be noted that all the areas designated as the scenes of the struggle are volcanic zones. The ancients imagined that earthquakes, volcanic eruptions, and seaquakes were due to the Giants, whose movements or breathing were attempts to break free from the mountains or islands that oppressed them and caused these upheavals.

Analysis and Understanding

1) Who were the leaders of the Giants?
2) What were the names of the other Giants?
3) Where did the battle of the Giants against the gods take place?
4) Why did Zeus call his son Heracles to the fight?
5) How was Alcyoneus defeated?
6) What did the giant Enceladus do?
7) Who emerged victorious at the end of this fight?
8) What does "Campi Flegrei" mean?
9) What is bradyseism?
10) What did the ancient Greeks believed produced the thermal phenomena?

Reworking and Production

1) Explain in your (own) words why the ancients imagined that most of the natural phenomenawas were due to the movements of the Giants.

2) Write a short dialogue imagining how Zeus convinces Hercules to fight by his side.

3) Build a table with the names of the Giants on the left and the deities who defeated them on the right.

Theogony of Hesiod

Teogonia means "the origin of the gods." It is said that from Chaos (the Void) arose Gaea, the Earth, from which Tartarus (Hell or the underworld) immediately broke away. Then Eros, Love, appeared, the force which tends to ensure that the elements are joined together.

Gaea bore Uranus (the mountains and the clear sky) and Pontus (the sea); from Chaos Erebus (darkness, the first darkness) and the Night were born. From Notte (Night) Destiny, Death, Discord, Old Age and the terrible Moire, or Fates, arbiters of life and death, were born.

There were twelve Titans, six males and six females. The most famous of them are Oceanus (the river that surrounds the globe and is the father of all the rivers), Tethys (moisture), Ceo (the sky), Cronos (time), Rea (movement and duration), Iapetus (the father of Prometheus, who will be discussed below) and Mnemosyne (memory).

There were three Cyclopes (the term means "round eyes"): Bronte, Sterope and Arge (Thunder, Lightning and Flash). Each had a single eye on his forehead.

Cotto (progenitor of the Cotti, the Thracian people), Briareus (Strong) and Gyges (born from the Earth) were the Centimani. They represented the overwhelming forces of nature, such as earthquakes and seaquakes.

Oceanus and Tethys fathered the nymphs Oceanids, Hyperion (the god of light) and Tea (the radiant), who in turn fathered Helios (the sun), Selene (the moon) and Eos (the dawn).

From Gaea and Ponto the sea gods were born: Nereus (calm sea), father of the Nereids (sea nymphs) and Thaumas (the majestic sea), father of Iris (the rainbow) and the Harpies (the storm winds), plus other minor deities.

Analysis and Understanding

1) Which god was born first from Chaos? What does his name mean?
2) What separated from Gaea?
3) Which deity, that is the force that joins the elements, appeared then?
4) Which gods were born from the Night?
5) Who were the Fates, and what were their names?

6) How many Titans were there? Write at least five of the most famous names.

7) What did the Centimani represent?

8) Who was Hyperion?

9) What is the name of the deity of the Moon?

10)   And that of the rainbow?

Reworking and writing

1) The myths about the genesis, that is, the birth of the world, are extremely confusing and vague. A number of beings, sometimes monstrous or immortal, crowd around the main deities, participating in this world still being formed. Can you tell if the scenarios in which these events take place are well defined or, on the contrary, undefined?

And if the time in which they take place is a delimited time or, on the contrary, broad and not well delimited?

2) Often, creation myths, as we have said, give great importance to "water". Why do you think this happens? Do a search on the "primordial soup".

Theogony in Ovid

Then there is a myth about the origin of the gods told by Ovid in his work "The Metamorphosis". It is called this because it talks about the changes in plants, animals or constellations endured by humans.

These occur for various reasons: either because men and women are saved by a god or goddess who take them away from danger, or as punishment from the gods for having behaved badly or too proudly against the gods themselves, or to make them immortal, as in the case of the constellations, and visible for eternity to everyone in heaven.

In this work, therefore, it is said that the god of all things (Ovid says that whoever it may be, some call him Nature), appeared in Chaos and separated the earth from the sky, the water from the land and the air of the area above from the lower zone.

He continued this process, separating the hot lands from the cold and temperate, forming plains and mountains, raising plants.

He created the stars and assigned to the four winds the directions in which they were to blow, then made the animals of the sea and of land, then the sun, the moon and the planets.

Finally he created man.

But Ovid also says that there is another myth about the creation of man, namely that of Prometheus, son of the Titan Iapetus, who modeled water and clay into human form.

This was then animated by divine elements wandering in space.

It's interesting to note that the creation myth by means of clay and water recalls the Babylonian poem Enuma Elish, where it is said that the god Marduk created the human race by mixing the earth with the blood of Kingu, a defeated enemy. In some ancient texts it is the Archangel Michael who carries the earth and water required to create Adam, the first man, to Jehovah, the God of the Jewish people.

Even in Genesis (origin), the first book of the Bible, there is the description of the creation of man by God from the dust of the earth.

In the Bible there is a further act of God: blowing into the nostrils of the newly created man to instill the breath of life in him.

These references to similar situations help us understand how relationships between ancient peoples must have been rather close, and provoked mutual influences even in religious matters.

Analysis and Understanding

1) What does the term "metamorphosis" mean?
2) In the work of Ovid, why are humans sometimes transformed into plants, animals or constellations?
According to Ovid's myths, did only one god give rise to creation or was it more than one god?
4) Who created man, modeling him from water and mud according to the Greek myth?
5) Who was the father of Prometheus?
6) What is the title of Babylonian poem that speak of the world's creation?

7) Who was Marduk?

8) Who led the land and water required to create Adam?

9) What does 'Genesis' mean?

10) How do we explain the presence of similar myths from various ancient peoples?

Reworking and Writing

1) This myth tells us that a god separated the waters from the earth, the earth from heaven, and top from bottom. In fact, the ancients believed that the earth was a disk surrounded by water. Only later, and slowly, it was realized that it was shaped like a sphere. After finding more about this, write a short essay about the arguments.

2) Find the differences in the two versions of the Biblical Book of Genesis and write a short essay on the subject.

Genesis (the Greek word meaning "birth, creation, origin") is the first book of the Christian Bible and is part of the Old Testament, namely the Pentateuch, which is the name of the first five books.

Long considered as having been written by Moses himself, now many scholars would agree that it is a collection of writings from various authors, which have been gathered over a long period of time.

The Bible is therefore a historical book, but of religious history, so its language is often symbolic.
In the Biblical book of Genesis the creation tale is told twice, with notable differences.
In the first version, the animals are created before and after man, and man is created with the woman.
In the second version, however, first the man is created and then all the animals, then finally the woman is created from the man's rib.

First version
Genesis, Chapter 1
• [11] Then God said, "Let the land produce vegetation: seed-bearing plants and trees on the land that bear fruit with seed in it, according to their various kinds."

• [21] So God created the great creatures of the sea and every living thing with which the water teems and that moves about in it, according to their kinds, and every winged bird according to its kind.

• [25] God made the wild animals according to their kinds, the livestock according to their kinds, and all the creatures that move along the ground according to their kinds. And God saw that it was good.

• [27] So God created mankind in his own image, in the image of God he created them; male and female he created them.

Second version
Genesis, Chapter 2
• [7] Then God formed a man from the dust of the earth and breathed into his nostrils the breath of life, and the man became a living being.
• [9] God made all kinds of trees grow out of the earth, trees that were pleasing to the eye and good for food.

• [18] God said, "It is not good for the man to be alone. I will make a helper suitable for him."

• [19] Now God had formed out of the ground all the wild animals and all the birds in the sky. He brought them to the man to see what he would name them; and whatever the man called each living creature, that was its name.

• [20] ... but the man did not found a helper fit for him.

• [21] So God caused the man to fall into a deep sleep; and while he was sleeping, he took one of the man's ribs and then closed up the place with flesh.

• [22] Then the Lord God made a woman from the rib he had taken out of the man, and he brought her to the man.

THE OLYMPIANS

The Twelve Olympian Gods

Greek religion is polytheistic, as we have seen. It believes in the existence of many gods. According to the Greeks, gods lived on Mount Olympus, the highest mountain in Greece.

Its top was often covered by clouds, which made it even more mysterious and fed the fertile imagination of the ancients.

Gods had not only the appearance of men, but also their character, with all the typical strengths and weaknesses of mortals.

Each god or goddess had his or her history, symbolism and field of action.

Specific human characteristics were attributed to each of them.

So Athena was the goddess of intelligence, Aphrodite of beauty, Hephaestus the expert in the art of metalworking, etc.

As for Zeus, the ruler of the gods, we must say he was a powerful and influential lord of the world, but had a number of weaknesses and passions that made him similar to mortals.

The most striking defect related to Zeus is his infidelity, which often infuriates his divine consort, who, however, finds a thousand ways to get revenge.

For the Greeks there is not a clear division between gods and men; the gods often participate in human affairs, speak in favor of or against this or that mortal man, change the course of events, or take care about the fate of this or that character.

Often they quarrel among themselves about interventions against their favorites, for the inconvenient positions, for the hostility shown towards anyone on earth.

They aren't above everything and everyone - rather they are deeply involved in the human sphere.

All these events feed artistic and, in particular, literary works, from the oldest, handed down initially in oral form, to the most modern, those composed by authors of our time, who still draw the ever-living heritage of these ancient myths.

There were twelve main gods who lived on mount Olympus: Zeus, Hera, Poseidon, Hermes,

Aphrodite, Ares, Estia, Phoebus, Artemis, Hephaestus, Demeter and Athena.

Later, however, Hestia gave up her place to Dionysus, to get away from the quarrels between the gods. She preferred not to have a fixed abode, knowing that because she was well-liked by everyone, she went would be welcomed wherever she went.

That's why our list of "twelve" Olympians actually contains "thirteen" of them.

To these others were added, some of whom were no less important: Pan, Persephone, the Dioscuri, Elio, Aeolus, etc., who presided over many aspects of human life, the atmosphere and other phenomena.

Analysis and Understanding

1) What does polytheistic religion mean?
2) Why were the most important gods called "Olympic"?
3) What does the term "anthropomorphism" mean?
4) What human characteristics did the Greek gods have?
5) Who was the ruler of the gods?
6) What was his biggest fault?
7) What were the names of the twelve Olympic Gods?

8) Who then took the place of Hestia on Olympus?

9) Were there other deities in addition to the Olympic Gods?

10) What were the names of some of these lesser gods?

Reworking and Writing

1) In history you studied the Egyptian religion which is equally polytheistic. Egyptian gods have "zoomorphic" characteristics, i.e., they are presented as having some animal-like features.
Do a quick search for different Egyptian gods, specifying which animal is used to depict each of them.

2) Do a quick search for the first monotheistic religion of the ancient world.
If you do not know the meaning of "monotheistic", first look it up in the dictionary.

Zeus

Zeus was the god of heaven, the Lord of the Olympian gods, the gods who lived on Mount Olympus, and also the undisputed king of mortals.
He was also the god of rain, the collector of the clouds the dispenser of the lightning, and in

command of all atmospheric phenomena, including good weather.

The celestial phenomena controlled by him contained divine signs, that were interpreted by the oracles.

The term "oracle" means either people or priests who predicted the future, or the prophecies themselves.

His symbols were the eagle and the oak tree.

Zeus was the youngest son of the god Cronos, who as we know devoured his children for fear of being overthrown as prophesied, and of the goddess Rhea, who saved him by hiding him in Crete and making her husband eat a stone wrapped in swaddling clothes instead of her newborn.

Once he was grown, and helped by the Cyclopes and Centimani, he ousted his father and his uncles, the Titans, as it is told in Titanomachia (see above), and saved his brothers and sisters who had been swallowed.

His siblings were immortal and therefore came out safe and sound from the stomach of Cronos.

Zeus then had to face the terrible Giants, whom he defeated with the help of the other gods and Heracles, as we have also seen.

Finally he had to fight Typhon, the monster son of Tartarus and Earth, who was eventually destroyed.

After these victories he was recognized as the lord of the world and together with his two brothers decided on the division of the Three Kingdoms: to

Zeus fell the domain of the sky, to Poseidon governance of the sea, and to Hades, control of Tartarus, the dark underworld.

Hestia, the goddess of the hearth and Demeter, the goddess of the harvest, were two other sisters of Zeus.

In Homeric poems, Zeus is represented as a just and merciful god, husband of Hera, with whom he had Ares, the god of war, Hebe, the goddess of youth, Hephaestus, the god of fire and Ilizia, the goddess of birth.

But in Greek religion, as we said previously, the gods are seen with all the vices and virtues of men.

Zeus is in fact guilty of numerous marital infidelities, which made his wife Hera jealous, who then often took vengeance.

It was thought that he could see and govern all things, taking into account everything that men were doing.

The kings of the earth were considered his descendants, and the Greek city-states were under his protection.

Together with the sky and the earth, Zeus also protected the domestic house, maintained the peace and the assets of every household, and sanctified marriage.

Also he maintained friendship between men, granted aid to those who needed it, such as supplicants and foreigners, and oversaw oaths.

Two of the four major Panhellenic festivals were dedicated to him.

They brought together all the Greeks, and they were the Olympic Games (which were held in Olympia, in Ilia) and the Nemean Games (celebrated in Nemea, in Argolis).

However, despite his power, even Zeus was subjected to Fate, or Destiny, a mysterious and powerful force, which no one could oppose.

Analysis and understanding

1) Of which weather phenomena was Zeus the king?
2) What were his symbols?
3) Who was his father? Who saved him by hiding him in a cave in Crete?
4) Against whom did Zeus fight?
5) Where were the Titans cast?
6) Who was Typhon?
7) Which kingdom was given to Zeus in the division of the world?
8) What children did he have with his wife?
9) To what were the celebrations dedicated?
10) To whom did he have to submit, even though he was so powerful?

Reworking and writing

1) Do a search on the paintings and sculptures representing Zeus.

2) Try to depict the king of the gods sitting on his throne, in his home on Mount Olympus.

3) Write a brief dialogue that represents Rhea offering her husband a stone wrapped in swaddling clothes, to deceive him and thus save the baby Zeus.

Hera

She was the wife of Zeus and the queen of the gods, the daughter of Cronos and Rhea. According to tradition she was born on the island of Samos. Her children were Ares, the war god, Hephaestus, the god of fire, and daughters Hebe, the goddess of youth and Ilizia, the goddess of birth.

She was the protector of marriage and of married women. She was jealous and vindictive; she did not forget any offenses against her and she was happy to persecute her enemies.

Her anger after the Judgment of Paris is famous. He, the son of King Priam of Troy, when having to decide who would get a golden apple on which was written "to the most beautiful," had to choose from

Hera, Athena and Aphrodite, the goddess of beauty and love; he chose Aphrodite. From then on Hera helped the Greeks against the Trojans, until their final defeat, despite the fact that Zeus supported of latter.

The animal sacred to this goddess was the peacock. Plants dedicated to her were the helichrysum, pomegranate and lily. She is often represented with a tiara and a veil, as a majestic and solemn woman.

Her power was enormous; she could give the gift of prophecy to anyone who wanted it, man or animal. As is the case among humans, even the gods bickered among themselves, and Zeus and Hera did it often. Only that Hera, for fear of being electrocuted by the lightning bolts of Zeus, knew how far she could go, and when she had to submit instead. So sometimes she was content to weave intrigues against the unfortunates who had offended her.

One day Zeus became so arrogant and insufferable that all the gods, led by this same goddess, decided to take him prisoner and to elect another in his place. While the god was sleeping, they surrounded him and bound him with leather ropes, knotted a hundred times. Zeus awoke, screamed and threatened revenge, but they laughed and did not care, because they had hidden his lightning bolts, which were his terrible weapon, in a safe place.

But the Nereid Thetis, to avoid a war on Olympus, went to call Briareus, one of the giants with a hundred hands. He managed to untie all the knots in a very short time and to free Zeus. To punish Hera, who was the organizer of the conspiracy, the king of the gods hung her from the sky by two gold bracelets. He was eventually moved with compassion and released his wife, making the other gods promise they would not rebel again.

He punished Phoebus and Poseidon, forcing them to work for a year for a mortal, King Laomedon, who was to build the walls of Troy, but forgave all other gods, because they had been instigated by them.

Analysis and Understanding

1) According to Greek tradition, where was Hera born?
2) What was she the protector of?
3) Why did she help the Greeks in their famous war with the Trojans?
4) What animal was sacred to her?
5) Why was Zeus at one point tightly bound by the other gods?
6) What did the Nereid Thetis do?
7) Who liberated Zeus from the leather cords which were holding him prisoner?
8) What was the punishment Zeus inflicted on Hera?

9) Before releasing Hera, what did Zeus make her promise?

10) What two gods were punished by being sent to earth to work for a mortal?

Reworking and Writing

1) Compose a short text imagining a dialogue between Paris and the three goddesses: Hera, Athena and Aphrodite.

2) Find information about the Trojan War and write a summary of the major events.

3) The site of the ancient city of Troy was discovered by Heinrich Schliemann. Do research on the subject.

Poseidon

He was the son, as Zeus and Hades were, of the Titan Cronos and Rhea. After deposing their father Cronos, the three gods divided the world, drawing lots from a helmet to know who would control the domains of the sky, the sea, and the underworld. To Poseidon fell the realm of the sea, where he quickly built a beautiful underwater palace.

Needing a wife, he first courted the Nereid Thetis, but when he learned of the existence of a prophecy that a son generated by her would be more famous than his father, he changed his mind and made Thetis marry Peleus, a mortal. He then fell in love with another Nereid, Amphitrite, but she would not accept his courting and fled to Mount Atlas. Poseidon sent several messengers to her, including Dolphin, who convinced Amphitrite to accept Poseidon. To thank Dolphin, the god made him immortal by putting him between the stars of the sky.

Then the wedding was celebrated, and from this was born Triton, whose upper body was human in form, while the lower part was fish-shaped. He announced the arrival of the god of the sea with a horn-shaped shell, which could also be used to calm the storm.

As Zeus, Poseidon also had numerous love affairs, from which many children were born, often strong and cruel, like the hunter Orion or the cyclops Polyphemus. He fathered Pegasus, the winged horse, from the Gorgon Medusa.

There are many legends around the figure of the god of the sea; for example that he fought the goddess Athena to gain control of the city of Athens, but to no avail.

After helping the king Laomedon, with the god Phoebus, to build the walls of Troy, he did not receive the agreed fee, and retaliated by sending a sea monster that devastated the region.

He hated Odysseus, who had blinded his son Polyphemus, and he punished the hero by hindering his trip back to his homeland, Ithaca.

Poseidon rode on a golden chariot drawn by white horses with golden manes and hooves of bronze and he was always surrounded by other sea gods. With his trident he caused earthquakes, sea storms and shipwrecks. As sacred animals he had the horse, the bull and the dolphin. The pine tree was also deemed sacred to Poseidon.

The Greeks, who were great sailors, built many temples in his honor. On Isthmus of Corinth they built a magnificent temple, where the Isthmian Games took place. These gathered athletes and spectators from all the cities of Greece. In Magna Grecia (the Great Greece) Poseidonia arose, the city of Poseidon, which today we call Paestum.

Analysis and Understanding

1) What kingdom fell to Poseidon?
2) Where did he build his magnificent palace?
3) Why did Poseidon stop courting the Nereid Thetis?
4) Who did he then marry?
5) Who persuaded Amphitrite to accept Poseidon as a husband?
6) Who was Triton?

7) Why did he hinder Odysseus's return to his homeland, Ithaca?

8) Against which king, who had not kept his promise, did he send a sea monster?

9) Why did the Greeks build many temples in honor of Poseidon?

10) How did he move within his marine realm?

Reworking and Writing

1) From the Nereid Thetis and the mortal Peleus a famous hero was born. Do a search on the subject.

2) Using a history book to help you, write a short essay on "Magna Grecia".

3) Do a quick search on the foundation of Paestum in today's Campania.

Hermes

Hermes was the son of Zeus and the Pleiade Maia, daughter of the Titan Atlas. He was born on Mount Cyllene, in Arcadia, and was precocious from the very beginning. The legend says that as a newborn he jumped out of the crib and went in search of adventure.

He is remembered as the inventor of the lyre, the stringed musical instrument (some say with three, some four, some seven strings), that he fashioned from a tortoise shell.

It is said that one day he went to a camp where a herd of cattle, belonging to the god Phoebus, was was grazing and, without thinking too much about it, he decided to steal some. To leave no traces, he made shoes for the horse from bark and tied them with woven grass. Then he took away the animals.

The god Phoebus noticed the theft, but although he tried in every way he could not find the culprit. So he offered a reward to those who would help. Silenus and satyrs of his entourage immediately began to search. At first, they had no luck. Then one day, they heard sweet music that they had never heard before, coming out of a cave. They asked a nymph outside cave what that sweet sound was. Thus, they learned that a boy had built a new musical instrument, with a turtle shell and the innards of a cow. They noticed two bovine skins hung out to dry in front of the cave. At that moment Phoebus came and recognized the skins of the animals as belonging to his herd.

He asked for explanations from Maia, the nymph mother of the little one, who showed the god as her son, still in diapers, blissfully asleep. Actually the cunning Hermes was only pretending to sleep.

However, Phoebus, who was not fooled, decided to punish him and led him onto Olympus, in the presence of Zeus, who by the way was his father.

Here, after much insistence, the little one confessed, but Phoebus decided to leave the herd in exchange for the new musical instrument Hermes had created, and it was so. Later, while he was with the grazing cows, Hermes took a reed which grew in a creek and created a whistle. He then began to play a sweet melody. Phoebus heard it and he again wanted to take ownership of the instrument, giving in exchange his golden stick with which he could gather the herds.

From that day Hermes also became the god of herdsmen and shepherds. He asked, however, also to learn the art of divination and Phoebus advised him to contact the Trie, his old attendants who lived on Mount Parnassus. They taught him to predict the future by observing the arrangement of stones placed in a container of water.

Zeus, who was proud of his son, but who also had to listen to the complaints of the other gods, those who were robbed of the things they cared most for (the hammer and the anvil of Hephaestus, the belt of Aphrodite, the trident of Poseidon, the sword of Ares) sent for Hermes and scolded him, then made him promise that he would never steal again.

But as he realized that Hermes was ingenious and eloquent, he appointed him messenger of the gods and patron of businesses, travelers and business contracts. To help in these tasks he gave him winged sandals, which could take him anywhere with the highest speed. Then he gave him a round hat to shelter him from the rain, and a stick of gold adorned with white ribbons, (or snakes, as other sources say).

Hermes also had the task of accompanying the souls of the dead to the underworld, of protecting athletes and stadiums, and of bestowing good luck and wealth. He was also the patron of thieves and had magical powers over sleep and dreams.

It is said that he invented astronomy, the musical scale, scales for measuring capacity, and even boxing and olive cultivation.

Analysis and Understanding

1) Where was the god Hermes born, and what did he do just after he was born?
2) What did he invent and what did he use to build it?
3) Which god stole the oxen?
4) What did he do to leave no traces of his actions?
5) Who helped Phoebus to find the herd?
6) What other musical instrument did he invented and how did he build it?
7) What had he stolen from the other gods?
8) Why did Zeus appoint him the messenger of the gods?
9) What did Zeus give him after naming him the messenger of gods?

10) What is it said Hermes invented?

Reworking and Writing

1) The lyre or harp is an instrument widely used by poets in ancient times, with which they accompanied themselves as they recited their poems. Find the meaning of the term "lyric poetry" and why it is called so.

2) Draw objects that Hermes stole from other gods.

3) How would you describe the character of the god Hermes, given the adventures in which he was the protagonist?

Aphrodite

Aphrodite was the goddess of love and beauty. She was born, according to legend, of the sea foam.

Zeus made her marry Hephaestus, the blacksmith god, but there are tales of numerous amorous adventures on the part of the goddess: with Ares, god of war, Hermes, messenger of the gods, Dionysus, god of wine, and Poseidon, god of the sea.

The goddess also fell in love with Adonis, a beautiful young man, who was also beloved of the goddess Persephone, queen of the underworld.

Zeus was called upon to decide which of the two goddesses should be awarded Adonis, but refused to do so, hoping to avoid problems.

He instead commissioned the muse Calliope to act as arbiter. She ruled that the two goddesses had equal rights to the boy, but also that these rights were to be enjoyed during separate periods of time in which each goddess could be alone with Adonis, as well as some time alone for the young man apart from either goddess. He was to be four months with Aphrodite, four months with Persephone, and four alone.

In fact, the figure of Adonis is connected with the god of vegetation, it is for this we have the division of the seasons (in Greece and in the surrounding regions, the sacred year of the goddess was divided into three parts, then reduced to two, beginning with the equinoxes or solstices).

But Aphrodite did not respect the agreements. Persephone then complained to Ares, making him jealous. The god then turned him into a wild boar and snapped at Adonis while he was hunting, making him die under the eyes of Aphrodite. The legend says that from his blood anemones, delicate flowers, arose.

But the goddess, in tears, asked Zeus to let Adonis spend the darkest days of the year in the company of Persephone in the underworld, and in the summer season to return with her. The king of the gods, who had immense powers, as we know, agreed.

Aphrodite then also fell in love with a mortal, Anchises, King of the Dardanians. She gave birth to a son destined to great deeds, Aeneas. After the destruction of Troy, he left for Italy, to found Roman civilization. His son Iulus founded Alba Longa, from whose kings Romulus and Remus descended, as the famous legend tells.

In the West, the cult of Aphrodite had the largest center in Erice, Sicily, where there was a sanctuary dedicated to the goddess.

She was considered the goddess of spring in bloom. The roses, the myrtle and the apple tree were sacred to her. She was represented adorned with roses and myrtle, on a chariot drawn by sparrows, doves and swans.

She had a magic belt that made anyone wearing it invisible. Once she even lent it to Hera, when she had to regain her husband Zeus. She was often accompanied by the Graces and the genies of craving and persuasion, almost as if to say that seductive talk deceives even the heart of the wise, as the great poet Homer says.

Aphrodite was favored over Hera and Athena in the famous "Judgment of Paris". Legend says that at the wedding of Peleus and Thetis (the future parents of Achilles, the Greek hero who is discussed in the Iliad), all the gods were invited, except Eris, the goddess of Discord.

Eris showed up in revenge at the banquet with a golden apple with the inscription "To the most beautiful", and tossed it among the goddesses. Aphrodite, Hera and Athena began to quarrel over ownership of the apple; then they turned to Zeus to decide. The god decided that it would be Paris, a Trojan prince, son of Priam and Hecuba, and considered the most beautiful man in the world, to decide to which of the three goddesses would go the title of the most beautiful.

To be chosen the goddess Hera offered Paris the command of Asia Minor. Athena instead said that, if he chose her, she would give him fame, wisdom and glory in battle. Aphrodite promised him the love of the most beautiful woman among mortals, namely Helen, wife of Menelaus, king of Sparta.

Paris chose this gift and gave the golden apple to Aphrodite, but the abduction of Helen then gave rise to the famous Trojan War, during which, after countless battles and duels, Paris killed Achilles. Paris then was killed in turn by Philoctetes with the enchanted bow that Heracles had given to him.

During the war of course Aphrodite sided with the Trojans, protecting Paris and also Aeneas, who was the son that the goddess had had with Anchises.

Analysis and Understanding

1) How was Aphrodite born according to legend?
2) Whom did Zeus make her marry?
3) With which mortal did Aphrodite and Persephone fall in love?
4) With which god can Adonis be identified?
5) What was born from the blood of Adonis according to legend?
6) To which famous hero did Aphrodite and Anchises give birth?
7) What was the main center of worship of Aphrodite in the West?
8) What property did the belt of Aphrodite have?
9) To which of the three goddesses did Paris give the golden apple?
10) Why did the goddess side with the Trojans during the Trojan War?

Reworking and Writing

1) In the Aeneid, the famous poem by the poet Virgil, Roman civilization descends from Aeneas. How?

2) Write a quick summary of the legend of Romulus and Remus.

Ares

Ares was the son of Zeus and Hera. He was the god of war and had as his sister Eris, Discord, who always stirred up new wars spreading enmity, rivalry and jealousy. He did not favor one city over another, but he was always ready to fight, on one side or the other, as he decided at the time. Athena also presided over war, but cleverly and strategically, while Ares was the god of uncontrolled and bloody violence.

He was not very well liked by the other gods, even by Zeus and Hera, for he had a violent and quarrelsome temper. He got along only with Aphrodite, as we have already said, and with Hades, the god of the underworld, who welcomed the souls of those who had died bravely in battle.

However, Ares wasn't always victorious. Athena beat him twice, and he took refuge on Olympus. Heracles also once won against him.

In fact, legend has that Cicno, a son of Ares, was very violent and bloody, and was building a temple with the bones and skulls of passersby that he had killed. But Heracles killed him, sparking the ire of his father Ares, who fought with the hero, but was defeated and humiliated.

The god wore bronze armor and travelled on a chariot drawn by four immortal horses. The dog and the vulture were his sacred animals, as were the barn owl, the owl, and the woodpecker. His symbols were the spear and the torch. His aides, when he participated in war, were the devil of the noise of the battle, the spirits of battle and the spirits of murder.

His children by Aphrodite were Terror and Fear. With the goddess of beauty he also fathered Eros, the god of love, Anteros, the god of reciprocated love, and Harmony. It seems strange that the gods of love and harmony could be born as children from the god of war. Perhaps this would mean that within a state waging war, there was a lot more harmony than there was in peacetime.

Also the Amazons were daughters of Ares. They were warrior women, whom we find in many legends.

Later Ares become the god that could grant peace, for which purpose he could be relied upon.

It is also said that one day Aloadae, the children of Aloeo, who were called Otus and Ephialtes, assaulted Olympus, and managed to chain the god and lock him in a bronze vase. But the stepmother of the two giants, the beautiful Eribea, revealed to the god Hermes what the two had contrived. Then Hermes went to save Ares, finding him screaming and moaning. Poor Ares was injured very badly, but Hermes finally freed him and he was able to return to Olympus. The goddess Artemis then punished Otus and Ephialtes, so that they would kill one another. In fact, she turned into a deer and ran between them; the two, who were experienced hunters, threw their spears so as not to miss their prey, but in the end they killed each other with them.

Analysis and Understanding

1) Who was the sister of Ares?
2) What was the difference between Ares and Athena, also goddess of war?
3) Why was he not very well liked by the other gods?
4) What was his son Cicno building?
5) Who were his helpers in the battles?
6) What children did he have with Aphrodite?
7) Who were the Amazons?
8) What were the names of the Aloadae and what did they do to Ares?
9) Who saved him?
10) Who punished Otus and Ephialtes?

Reworking and Writing

1) Do a quick search on Hades, the Underworld.

2) List the various sons of Ares and their characteristics.

3) Draw Ares imprisoned in the bronze vase, explaining the drawing with a caption.

Hestia

Hestia was the goddess of the fire that burned in the hearth. She was the eldest daughter of Cronos and Rhea, sister of the other gods of Olympus: Demeter, Hera, Hades, Poseidon and Zeus.

When her father, Cronos, was dethroned and the power passed to Zeus, Hestia swore to remain faithful to her brother.

She did not wish to marry, although she had many suitors. Zeus was glad, because he avoided the possibility that someone else could aspire to the throne (most gods married, more children were born and the many of them could have taken his place as king of the gods).

Then he rewarded her for preserving the peace of Olympus, promising that the first victim of any public sacrifice would be dedicated to her; and so it was, when they sacrificed to the gods, the first offering was always to Hestia.

She was the goddess of the hearth, both in the home and in public places. In all private homes the hearth was considered a kind of altar at which to make sacrifices. Additionally, there were fires hearths in public places and each city had a brazier in the most important building, most often the main temple, where the sacred fire was burning to the goddess. This fire was never to go out and was continuously monitored.

The goddess represented family security, household serenity and also the sacred duty of hospitality. She was considered the protectress of all Greek cities because they were seen as an extension of the family community. If the fire, which was considered sacred, was extinguished, either accidentally or in mourning, then they rekindled it immediately using flint.

She was venerated because she was good-natured, honest and generous and also because it is said she invented the art of building houses.

There was the custom that the bride, or the bride's mother, would take fire from the hearth of the house of origin and take it into the new house in order to consecrate it.

Another ritual took place after the birth of a child. Five days after birth, the father took him in his arms and went five times around the fire, as a sign of the child's acceptance into the family.

Even those who went to found colonies in other parts of the world carried a lighted torch from the fire of the city from which they had departed, and this was used to start the fire in each temple or building in the town that they founded.

Hestia did not have a precise representation, because she didn't have a distinctive appearance, but was identified with fire, which has a changing aspect.

Her symbol was then the fire burning on circular braziers, in homes and cities. Even the temples dedicated to her were circular. Prayers were addressed to her before or after meals, and she was often invoked as a witness in private and public oaths.

She protected the supplicants, those who asked for help, because it was customary for this to take place by the fireside.

Analysis and Understanding

1) Who were the brothers and sisters of Hestia?
2) Of what was she the goddess?
3) How did Zeus reward her for not marrying?
4) Why was she considered the protector of all Greek cities?
5) How did they rekindle the fire, if it went out?
6) What did brides take to their new house?
7) What ritual did the father of a newborn carry out and why?
8) What did people carry with them when they founded new colonies?
9) Did the goddess have a very specific representation?

10) What was the shape of the temples dedicated to her?

Reworking and Writing

1) Search for information about the discovery of fire in prehistoric times.

2) Find depictions of circular temples dedicated to Hestia, then please make your own design.

Phoebus

Phoebus was the god of light. His name means "bright, shining". He drove the chariot of the sun and was also the god of music and prophecy. He was the leader of the Muses, the nine deities who presided over the arts, and thus he was the patron of poetry. His parents were Zeus and Leto. He was born, with his twin sister Artemis, on the island of Delos.

When the goddess Hera learned of the relationship of Zeus with Leto, in revenge she forbade her to give birth to children on any ground, continent or island. Leto then wandered on and on, until she stopped on the island of Delos. Delos had the distinction of floating on the waters of the sea, at the mercy of the currents, and therefore could not be considered a true island. Only after the two gods were born did Zeus fix it to the bottom of the sea, making it stable.

Legend has it that Artemis was born first and helped her mother to deliver the second child. Phoebus was born on the night of a full moon, which is why such nights were always consecrated to him. A few days after birth, the divine child asked for a bow and arrows, and the god Hephaestus granted his wish.

Then Phoebus went away from Delos to Mount Parnassus, where the serpent Python was. The serpent had offended his mother before he was born, and Phoebus struck him with his arrows. Python, wounded, then took refuge in Delphi, the city named after Delphine, a monster that was the companion of Python. Python was killed by the arrows of the god in the place where the famous oracle of Delphi would be built.

The cave, freed of the monster, became the place where a priestess, the Pythia, predicted the future. To commemorate the victory over the serpent Python in Delphi, the Pythian Games were celebrated every four years. However, the mother of Python, the goddess Gaea, punished Phoebus, sending him in exile for nine years to the king Admetus, a mere mortal. The god was forced to work for him as a shepherd but Admetus treated him so kindly that Phoebus later rewarded him (as described in the legend of Alcestis).

Another enterprise not very noble (even the gods sometimes misbehaved) of Phoebus was when he punished the satyr Marsyas. The satyr was guilty of having boasted of being better at playing the flute than Phoebus was in playing the lyre.

The god then angrily challenged him to a competition, saying that the winner would punish the vanquished in the way that he liked. The judgment was given to the Muses, who eventually ruled that the competition had ended equally because both had played delightfully.

Then Phoebus challenged Marsyas again; this time everyone would have to turn his instrument and sing. But the flute could not be played upside down, while the lira could be, thus the god won the race and took revenge in a very cruel, by flaying the poor satyr alive. He became the god of music and always played his lyre at banquets of the gods on Olympus.

Another legend relative to Phoebus speaks of Niobe, queen of Thebes. She had prided herself of having twelve sons, and derided Leto who had only two, and so Phoebus, with his sister Artemis, struck the woman with his arrows, killing her and her children.

Phoebus was also the god of medicine, and he taught his son Asclepius how to cure all ills. The god is represented with different symbols: the tripod (to remember the oracle of Delphi), the lyre, the bow and arrows, the laurel branch, the palm, the calf, the hawk and the crow.

Two famous quotes are engraved on the walls of the temple of Delphi: "Know thyself" and "Nothing to excess".

Analysis and Understanding

1) What does the name "Phoebus" mean?
2) Of which deity was he in charge?
3) Whose brother was he and where were they born?
4) Why was the island of Delos special?
5) Why was the full moon consecrated to Phoebus?
6) Where was Python killed and who was the Pythia?
7) For whom did he have to work as a shepherd?
8) Who won the competition with Marsyas?
9) Who served as referee in the competition against Pan?
10) Why did he punish Niobe together with Artemis?

Reworking and writing

1) Look up information about the oracle of Delphi and Pythias.

2) Explain, with the help of the teacher, what the two sentences "Know thyself" and "Nothing to excess" mean.

Artemis

She was the daughter of Zeus and Leto, and the twin sister of Phoebus She was the goddess of wild animals, the forest, the nature and hunting. Like her brother Phoebus, she has the power to cause sudden death and pestilence, but also the power to stop them.

She was worshiped as the goddess of birth because the legend said that she had helped her mother Leto during the birth of her brother Phoebus. She was also the goddess of the moon and was also called Cynthia (Cinzia) as she was born on Mount Cinto, in the island of Delos.

It is said that when she was just three years old, the goddess sat on the knees of her father Zeus and asked him to fulfill some of her desires: she said that she never wanted to get married, she wanted to have at her service a bow and arrows as her brother had, hunting dogs, deer to pull her wagon, and that she enjoyed the companionship of sixty ocean nymphs, who were to accompany her during the hunts, and twenty nymphs of the rivers. Then all the world's mountains and some city should be dedicated to her, but also she also said that a single city would have been enough, because she intended to live in the mountains.

Her father Zeus complied, and indeed not only granted a city, but thirty. He even named her the guardian of roads and ports. The goddess thanked her father and began to choose among the nymphs as her maids. Then she went to the island of Lipari, at the invitation of the god Hephaestus, where she visited the workshop of the Cyclops.

They were intent on building a manger for the horses of the sea god Poseidon; but the little goddess ordered them to stop. And in the time they were to devote to the job, they built for the goddess a silver bow and many arrows. What she wanted was immediately done.

Then she went to the god Pan, who gave her ten hounds, skilled hunting dogs. Then she captured four beautiful hinds, arming herself with golden bridles and attacking on a golden chariot.

It is said that one day the river god Alpheus fell in love with her and pursued her across the whole of Greece. The goddess took sheltered at Elis, a region of Greece. There, she soiled her face with white mud, doing the same to her Nymphs.

In this way, it wasn't possible to recognize which of the many girls was the goddess, and Alpheus had to give up the conquest and leave, accompanied by the laughter and derision of the Nymphs.

Another legend says that a bear had taken up the habit of going to the city of Brauron and that the people fed him, so that the animal quickly became docile and domesticated. But a girl began to annoy the bear, and it killed her. In turn the bear was killed by her brother, provoking the wrath of Artemis.

The goddess then proclaimed that the girls of the city must serve at her temple; since then the girls who were aged between five and ten years were to serve the goddess for one year in the sanctuary dedicated to her in the city of Brauron, and were called "small bears".

Her symbols were the deer, the bear and the cypress; she was often represented with a lion or a leopard, always with her quiver and arrows of silver, sometimes with a bow or a torch. The crescent was her recurring symbol, because she was identified with the goddess Moon (Luna), as we have already said.

Her temple in Ephesus, in Anatolia (modern Turkey) was famous, considered one of the seven wonders of the world. In this region she was worshiped primarily as a fertility goddess.

Analysis and Understanding

1) Who was Artemis's brother?
2) How was she also called, and why?
3) What things did she ask his father Zeus when she was just three years of age?
4) Which of her maids did she choose?
5) What did the Cyclopes and Hephaestus build for her?
6) Which ploy did she use to get rid of Alpheus?
7) Why did the maidens of Brauron have to serve the goddess for one year?
8) What were her symbols?
9) Why was the crescent one of his symbols?
10) Where was her most famous temple?

Reworking and Writing

1) Do a quick search on the Seven Wonders of the World.

2) Do you believe Artemis and her brother Phoebus got along, or not? Re-read the text on the god Phoebus to review, then write your observations.

3) Artemis was the goddess of hunting as well as animals and nature. Explain, in your own words, how these two aspects of her nature were linked in antiquity.

Hephaestus

Son of Zeus and Hera, he was the god of fire, metal and metallurgy. Thus, he became the blacksmith of the gods. When he was born he was so ugly that the legend says that his mother threw him down from Olympus.

He fell into the sea, where he was welcomed and brought up by the two sea gods Thetis and Eurynome. They hid him in an underwater cave, where Hephaestus arranged his first smithy, rewarding the two goddesses for their hospitality with jewels and numerous items of excellent workmanship.

After nine years, Hera met Thetis who was wearing a magnificent brooch. Immediately she wanted to know who the craftsman was who had made it.

She insisted so much that Thetis finally revealed the truth. The goddess Hera then decided to take him back to Olympus and she commissioned him to build her a golden throne.

But Hephaestus, in revenge for previous abandonment, built the throne with the invisible snares so that Hera, once seated, couldn't raise her body from the throne.

The cries of the goddess roused all the other inhabitants of Olympus, and Zeus sent Hermes to seek Hephaestus, to convince him to free his mother.

He, however, was not convinced, even when Zeus sent Ares to him. Only Dionysus, sent by Zeus, persuaded him as he had done before, getting him drunk with his exquisite wine.

Back to Olympus Hephaestus went and freed his mother. Hephaestus began to build many useful and beautiful objects for the gods, the shield of Zeus, Poseidon's trident, the helmet of invisibility for Hades, the chariot of the Sun, the bows and arrows of Artemis and Eros, the belt of Aphrodite, the helmet and the winged sandals of Hermes, many more weapons and armor for different heroes like Achilles and Aeneas.

He was also the builder of the first woman, Pandora.

To repay these wrongs, he was given Aphrodite in marriage (others say that he asked for Hera, in exchange for her release from the throne that kept her imprisoned).

One day he defended Hera from her husband, who had hung her in the sky after the goddess had rebelled against him.

Then, as punishment, an angered Zeus threw him back down from Olympus, and he is said to have dropped onto the island of Lemnos, fracturing his legs. He was rescued by the inhabitants of the island.

However, he was also immortal, but from that day onward he had to walk using crutches or a golden cane. But, he was a great artist and continued to work, having extraordinary strength in the muscles of his arms and shoulders.

From Lemnos, a volcanic island, the god then moved to Southern Italy; perhaps the Greek settlers brought his worship with them. Thus he was said to have had his forge under either Etna or the island of Lipari, which is equally volcanic.

His helper was the Cyclopes, the giant with a single eye.

The legend says that one day he built a group of fully mechanical young girls made of gold, who helped him in his work. They also knew how to speak, and carried the most difficult tasks.

Hephaestus then built twenty tables with three legs, and wheels of gold, which proved useful during the banquet of the gods, because they moved and returned by themselves to their place.

Often Zeus, in the guise of an eagle, created the dreaded thunderbolts in his forge.

His symbols are the hammer, anvil, and tongs; he is sometimes also represented with an ax.

He was the patron of all craftsmen, often worshiped together with the goddess Athena, and he was considered the father of Erichthonius, the legendary founder of the royal Athenian dynasty.

Analysis and Understanding

1) What happened to the newborn Hephaestus, and why?

2) By whom was he raised?

3) How did Hera see that he was still alive and had become a talented blacksmith?

4) How did Hephaestus retaliate against Hera after he was brought back to Olympus?

5) What objects did he build for the other gods?

6) Who was the first woman he built?

7) Which goddess did he marry?

8) On which island did he fall after Zeus hurled him from Mount Olympus?

9) Why were the tables that he built useful?

10) Why did Zeus often visit his workshop?

Reworking and Writing

1) The myth of Hephaestus recalls the importance that metallurgy, i.e. the art of metalworking, had among ancient peoples as well as modern ones. Do a search on the use and processing of metals from prehistoric times, seeking information about the age of copper, bronze and iron.

2) The cult of Hephaestus moved from the island of Lemnos, which is in Greece, to the island of Lipari, north of Sicily. Explain the reasons which led the Greeks to found colonies, first in the East and then in the West.

Demeter

She was a goddess of ancient origins, protector of vegetation, harvest and agriculture. Legend says that she gave mankind the agricultural techniques of plowing, sowing, harvesting.

She was represented as a solemn and majestic matron, with a crown of spikes of wheat on her head, a torch in one hand and a basket full of fruit in the other.

She was the daughter of Cronos and Rhea and sister of Zeus, but, according a legend, she had with him the daughter Kore ("the maiden"), also called Persephone ("she who brings destruction"), with whom she is closely connected. The two goddesses, the "divine couple", are the protagonists of the Eleusinian Mysteries, religious rituals that took place at Eleusis in the large sanctuary dedicated to Demeter.

According to an ancient orator, Isocrates, she would donate to men two very important things: cereals, which have made them so different from wild animals, and the Mysteries, which gave them hope of an afterlife.

Legend has it that one day the young Persephone, while picking flowers around a lake along with the Oceanusids Nymphs, walked away from them.

She was seen by Hades, the god of the Underworld, who decided to kidnap her and take her with him to the underworld by opening a hole in the ground. The screams of the young girl were heard by her mother, but she could not find her.

Demeter then wandered across Greece in search of her daughter, for nine days and nine nights, with two lighted torches, without eating or drinking, but it was in vain. Knocked down by a deep pain, the goddess decided to abandon her divine duties and retired to Eleusis, where she was received with generous hospitality. Because of her departure the rain no longer fell, and the ground did not give any fruit, so a terrible famine spread.

Then Zeus, yielding to the prayers of mortals and of the gods themselves, since men did not even have a thing to sacrifice to the gods, sent the god Hermes as messenger to Hades, in the underworld, ordering him to return Persephone to her mother.

Hades showed himself conciliatory, but he had devised a plan: before Persephone left to return to Earth, he made her eat some pomegranate seeds, which were magical. In fact, those who had eaten something in the realm of the dead could not get back into the realm of the living; so Persephone could not stay forever in the kingdom of men, but would have to return to the kingdom of the underworld.

When Demeter was reunited with her daughter, the land became fertile again and began to bear fruit. But when she learned that her daughter had eaten pomegranate seeds and could not stay with her forever, she fell into a deep sorrow. She promised that she would never return to Olympus, continuing to weigh her curse on earth.

Zeus then convinced his mother Rhea to intervene, and they came to an agreement: Persephone would spend three months (some say four, others six) in the underworld with Hades, as Queen of the Underworld, and the remaining months with her mother.

Demeter agreed, but decreed that when Persephone was in the realm of the dead nature would be asleep and the Earth would not bear fruits. However, in the remaining months, when Persephone was in the realm of the living the earth would wake up and produce abundant vegetation.

This is how the ancients explained so the difference between the autumn and winter and the spring and summer.

Before returning to Olympus, Demeter gave Triptolemus, a mortal who had helped her, wheat seeds and a plow, teaching him the art of agriculture.

Then she sent him on a winged chariot through all of Greece to teach all men what he had learned from her.

Then, it is said, that the goddess taught the art of cultivation even to Cinco, king of Scythia, the Central Asian region, but he refused to teach it in turn to his subjects, for which Demeter turned him into a lynx.

Another son was Pluto, the god of wealth.

The legend says that when he was born, the earth, to make him a bed, covered him with beautiful grain.

Still another son was Dionysus, the god of wine.

Demeter was beloved and celebrated throughout antiquity and had numerous temples dedicated to her; let's not forget that agriculture was one, if not the most important, of the main activities in the ancient world.

Analysis and Understanding

1) How was Demeter represented?
2) What was the daughter Kore's other name?
3) Where did the two goddesses, the "Divine Couple", worship?
4) Who kidnapped Persephone?
5) What happened to the earth when Demeter retired to Eleusis out of pain?
6) What did Persephone eat before returning to earth?
7) What was the agreement reached between Demeter and Hades?
8) To whom did Demeter teach the art of agriculture? What did she give him?
9) What was Cicno transformed into, and why?
10) What happened to the earth when Pluto was born?

Reworking and Writing

1) From hunting and gathering wild fruits, man starts to cultivate the land; the nomad becomes sedentary. Learn the theme of the birth of agriculture, the so-called "agricultural revolution".

2) Draw a map of the "fertile crescent", the area that includes Egypt and Mesopotamia and was the seat of the agricultural revolution.

Athena

She was the goddess of knowledge, wisdom, crafts, especially weaving, and of nobility in war.She was the favorite daughter of Zeus.
Her birth was very special.
The goddess came out of the head of Zeus, already adult and armed, because the father Zeus sired her with Metis, the goddess of prudence and wisdom. But the lord of the gods had heard a prophecy that the sons of Meti would become more powerful than their father. For fear of being ousted, he first transformed Metis into a fly and then swallowed her. The goddess was waiting for Athena; indeed she began to build a helmet and a robe for her. The noise she made with a hammer to build the helmet caused Zeus a terrible headache.
Then Hephaestus (or Prometheus, according to another version), by order of the king of the gods,

opened his head with an axe and from this Athena came, as mentioned above, adult and fully armed, crying strongly.

She was raised by Triton, the god of water, and grew up alongside his own daughter, who was named Pallas. The two girls practiced combat together, but while duelling, Athena unwittingly killed her friend. Distraught and saddened by what happened, she decided to build a statue with the features of Pallas, which was called the Palladium, and placed it near the statue of Zeus. To prove her pain, the goddess took the name of Pallas as sign of mourning, and so was often called Pallas Athena.

Athena was often designated as "sparkling-eyed" or "bright-eyed".

Her sacred animal was the owl, symbol of wisdom, with which she was often represented; the olive was the plant consecrated to her.

She is always depicted standing, with her armor, helmet, spear and a shield on which is fixed the head of the Gorgon Medusa, a monster that Perseus was able to defeat with the help of the goddess.

During the Trojan War, he fought alongside the Greeks, often along with Ares, but she differed from the god because he represented the force, war's fury, while she expressed the intelligence, tactics, and reason, even in the choices of war.

She was the protectress of all trades, of all the artsand all knowledge, and she was considered the protector of the state, of its laws and of the administration of justice.

Athena was also the patron of the city of Athens.

It is said that a dispute was born between her and Poseidon about which of them should be the deity responsible for the city, which did not yet have a name.

In the end, having the advice of the other gods, they found an agreement: each of them would give a gift to the inhabitants, and this, by choosing what gift they like more, would decided the patron deity.

Poseidon struck the ground with his trident, giving rise to a spring, but the water was not good to drink because it was brackish; some say he offered them a horse.

Instead Athena planted an olive tree, a plant that until then had not been cultivated, and taught the technique to extract the oil.

The citizens then chose the gift of Athena, because they had wood, oil and food, so the city took the name of the goddess.

In her honor they later built the Parthenon, the most famous temple in Greece, located on the Acropolis of Athens; it takes its name from the title Parthenos, Virgin, which meant that the goddess would never marry.

In the temple there was a huge statue of the goddess 11 meters high and made of gold and ivory by the famous sculptor Phidias. The statue was later destroyed.

Athena was also the protector of many heroes such as Heracles, Jason, Bellerophon and Achilles, but especially Odysseus.

Analysis and Understanding

1) How was Athena born?
2) In what way did Zeus transform Metis?
3) Who raised her? Who was Pallas?
4) What did Athena do to remember her friend?
5) By which names is she often designated?
6) What was her sacred animal?
7) What was depicted on her shield?
8) What was the city she protected?
9) What gift did the goddess offer to be chosen as the patron deity?
10) What is the Parthenon?

Reworking and Writing

1) We have seen that war in the world has two Greek gods who are responsible; explain in your own words why this happened. Then do a search on war in the ancient world, especially in the Greek world.

2) The Parthenon was built on the Acropolis of Athens in the age of Pericles, along with other famous monuments.
Write a brief summary of the Periclean age, using a history book to help you.

Dionysus

He is the Greek god that represents all that is instinctive, chaotic and irrational in life. He is the god of vegetation and fertility and especially the god of the vine and wine. According to myth, Dionysus was born in Thebes to Zeus and Semele. The goddess Hera, jealous, appeared in a dream to Semele and led her to ask the king of the gods to be admired in all his glory.

Zeus then appeared in the form of lightning and thunder, and the poor Semele remained thunderstruck because only the Olympian gods were allowed to see the true face of Zeus. The god saved the child to be born from the flames and sewed him in his thigh until the gestation was complete. Then he entrusted him to the nymphs of the mountain of Nysa, in Arcadia, who brought him up with honey. He grew up in an atmosphere of joy and gladness.

He became the god that cheered hearts and pleased people until he became great. During this period, Dionysius discovered the fruit of the vine, grapes, and learned to obtain, through fermentation, an exciting beverage, wine, unknown until then.

The goddess Hera, however, recognized him as the son of Zeus and punished him with madness. He then began traveling around the world to made known his discovery, accompanied by a procession of Satyrs and Bacchae, with his teacher, the old satyr Silenus.

Arriving in Egypt, he had to fight against the Titans, the giant beings who had stolen the scepter of the Egyptian king Ammon, and succeded in defeating them. Then he headed east, towards India, founding several towns along the way. He then returned to Greece, but first had to fight against the Amazons, women warriors, whom he finally defeated.

During his travels Dionysus often met people who would not recognize his divine nature, and therefore they were punished with death. We remember King Lycurgus, who wanted to imprison him, along with King Preto's daughters at Tiryns and the daughters of King Minia at Orchomenus. These last were driven mad and exchanged the son of one of them for a sacrificial victim, coming to kill him.

Even Orpheus, the oldest and most famous poet of Greece, who was devoted only to Phoebus and would not recognize the god of wine, was killed by the Maenads who tore apart his body. The Muse then gave him a decent burial.

But the most famous episode is that concerning Pentheus, the young king of Thebes. He opposed the cult of Dionysus, who had instead convinced all the women of Thebes to move to Mount Cithaeron and celebrate rites in his honor. Pentheus went so far as to have him imprisoned. A messenger came and told him that the women, at first peaceful and quiet had become furious and killed cattle and devastated villages.

Dionysus then suggested that the king go and spy on what was happening, but disguised as a woman so as not to be recognized, and he offered to drive him himself. So it happened, but Pentheus came to a sad end: he was torn to pieces by his own mother, Agave and by the other women; in his folly, she mistook him for a wild animal. Only later, when she returned to Thebes did Agave notice the terrible mistake committed and wept over her sad fate.

During one of his trips Dionysus was kidnapped by pirates who wanted to sell him as a slave in an eastern market. But the god turned the oars of the ship into snakes and stopped it with ivy and vines. Then he turned into a lion and conjured ghosts of wild animals, so the pirates went mad and threw themselves into the sea, becoming dolphins.

One day, landing on the island of Naxos, he found Ariadne, the girl who had helped Theseus to kill the Minotaur in Crete. She had been abandoned by Theseus on the island, or perhaps she had been forgotten. No one knows why, but the myths do not explain everything; they leave much to the imagination. Dionysus fell in love and took her with him, and from that day Ariadne was part of the festive procession of the god.

After having spread his cult all over the earth, the god went up to Olympus, where he was welcomed among the major deities. In fact, the mild Hestia gave him her place among the twelve Olympian gods, preferring to move away from the quarrels of the gods, and knowing that wherever she went she would be received with joy.

Finally, Dionysus descended into Hades to free his mother Semele. To convince Persephone to let her go, he gave the myrtle plant to the goddess of the underworld. In fact, his sacred plants were vines, ivy, pine, fig and myrtle. The animals dedicated to him were the raven, the bull, the panther, the lion, the snake and the donkey.

Analysis and Understanding

1) Who was the mother of Dionysus? Why was she struck by Zeus?
2) Which plant did the god discover in Arcadia?
3) How did he get wine from this?
4) Who formed his cortege?
5) Why did the god punish many people with death?
6) How was he freed from pirates? Into what were they turned?
7) Whom did he find on the island of Naxos?

8) How did the god behave with Ariadne?
9) Which goddess gave him her place among the twelve Olympic gods?
10) Which plant did he give to Persephone and why?

Reworking and Writing

1) Dionysus is primarily the god of wine; do a little research on how wine is made today.

2) A famous poem by Lorenzo the Magnificent speaks of Bacchus (which is the Latin name of Dionysus) and Ariadne. Look for it with the help of the teacher and comment on the poem.

OTHER GODS AND LEGENDS

Pan

He was a god with a human torso, but with the legs, horns, hooves, and bearded face of a goat. He did not live on Mount Olympus, but roamed the woods and forests, playing and dancing, accompanied by the Nymphs. He was the lord of the fields and woods at the hour of noon. He protected flocks and cattle, and mountain peaks were sacred to him; he had prodigious agility and was very fast at running and jumping.

He is said to have been the son of Hermes and Dryope, the nymph of the oak. At birth, he was so bad that his mother decided to leave him. Fortunately, Hermes saved him by wrapping him in a hare-skin and took him to Olympus to be among the other gods, who welcomed him with kindness, especially Dionysus, who was very amused and took him into his retinue. After that, he became one of the wine god's favorite companions, following him in his adventures, always cheerful.

One day Pan saw Syringe, the daughter of the river god Ladon, and fell in love; but the girl, when she saw him, ran away terrified and begged her father to turn her into anything so she could not be recognized by the god. Ladon then turned her into a reed that grew in a big swamp.

The god Pan tried in vain to recognize the girl in the countless reeds which grew there, and moved in the wind making a delicate sound. Not being able to get what he wanted, Pan then thought to build at least one musical instrument. So he cut marsh reeds into different lengths with which he created the legendary Pan Pipes, also called "syringe" in honor of the girl.

He then returned to wander the woods accompanied by the Nymphs, running and dancing, amusing themselves by scaring travelers who ventured into the woods with noises of inexplicable source.

It is said that he could not bear to be disturbed during the afternoon nap: if anyone dared to bother him, then the god uttered fearful cries that caused the "panic", a term that derives from his name, and which means a big fright.

Another curiosity: his name derives from a Greek word that means "feed", but also means "all", so the god would be the lord of all of nature, in all its aspects.

Analysis and Understanding

1) Where did the god Pan live?
2) Who was his mother?
3) Who saved him after his mother abandoned him? Where did he take him?
4) Which god welcomed him into his entourage?
5) With whom did Pan fall in love?
6) Into what was Syringe transformed?
7) What did Pan build, and with what, when he was unable to find the girl?
8) What could he not bear?
9) What does the term "panic" mean?
10) What does the term "pan" mean in Greek?

Reworking and Writing

1) We have already spoken of the lyre and the whistle, the two musical instruments invented by Hermes. With the panpipe, we have encountered a third. Search for other types of instruments in the Greek world during antiquity.

2) Find as many words as you can (at least ten) that in the English language are formed by the prefix "pan" meaning "all" (e.g. "Panhellenic").

Asclepius

He was the Greek god of medicine. He does not belong to the twelve Olympian gods, but he was venerated in many shrines scattered around the Mediterranean basin, including that of Pergamum in Asia Minor (modern Turkey) and that of Epidaurus in Greece.

According to legend, he was the son of Phoebus and Princess Coronis, whom the god saw while she bathed in a lake. The god fell in love, but having to move away, he entrusted the girl to a raven that had feathers white as snow. During the absence of Phoebus, not listening to reason, Coronis married a certain Ischi, and the raven had no choice but to go immediately to Phoebus to report the incident. The god punished the bird transforming his feathers from white to black because he had failed to keep Ischi from Coronis. Since then, all crows have had black plumage.

The sister of Phoebus, Artemis, to whom the god had complained, retaliated against him by killing Coronis with her arrows. The body of the unfortunate girl was already on the pyre to be burned when Phoebus realized that she was pregnant. Immediately he called for help from Hermes, who managed to save the baby.

He was given the name of Asclepius and learned the art of healing from both Phoebus and the centaur Chiron. Chiron raised him and taught him medical practices and the use of medicinal plants.

It is said that he healed the Proetides, King's Preto daughters, of their madness. They had become arrogant and had been punished by the gods, who drove them mad.

He cured the Fineidi, the sons of Phineas, of their blindness. They had been blinded by their own father because they had been unjustly accused by their stepmother. Finally, he healed the wounds of Heracles. But then his ambition grew, and he would even restore life to those who had lost it. He began to resurrect the dead: Orion, Hippolytus, Tyndareus and others.

The god of the underworld, Hades, complained of this to Zeus, who then shot Asclepius with one of his thunderbolts, because it was not possible to disrupt the laws of life and death. Phoebus, the father of Asclepius, in revenge, killed the Cyclopes, who made Zeus's thunderbolts, and left Olympus for a long time.

Later, however, Zeus again gave life to Asclepius, as had been predicted by a prophecy: according to this prediction he would become a god, would die and then come back to life.

He was represented as an old man with a long beard, carrying a stick with a snake coiled around it, because the snake was a symbol of change and rebirth (because every year it sheds its skin).

Festivals were dedicated to him, such as Asclepiee or Asclepiadee. Shrines dedicated to him consisted of a spring or well surrounded by a sacred grove, and a building that was used to house the sick. They spent the night there, and it was often said that this alone was enough to heal them. Other times they used drugs and real surgeries were also carried out.

His sacred animals, in addition to the serpent, were the dog, the goose and the rooster, which was the symbol of day and of the life reborn. The snakes (harmless ones), lived in freedom in his temples, without being disturbed. A snake, taken from the temple of Epidaurus, was brought into each new sanctuary dedicated to him.

Analysis and Understanding

1) Who were the parents of Asclepius?
2) Of what color were the feathers of the crow?
3) Why was the raven punished?
4) Who taught Asclepius the art of healing?
5) Why was he struck down by Zeus at a certain point?
6) How did his father Phoebus take revenge?
7) Why is the snake a symbol of change?
8) How were shrines dedicated to him made?

9) Why was his symbol also the rooster?
10) What did they bring to any new sanctuary?

Reworking and Writing

1) From the time of Asclepius and his priests, medicine had made many advances, but nothing could change if there is not beginning. Do a search on medicine and health in the ancient Greek world.

2) The ancients very often cured themselves with herbs by knowing the various properties of many numerous officinal plants, i.e., medicinal plants. Explain the meaning of medicinal plant and do some research on those more commonly used today.

Helios and the Chariot of the Sun

Helios was the sun god, son of the Titan Hyperion and Titaness Thea. He was the brother of Selene (Moon) and Eos (Dawn).
Every day, awakened by a rooster that was an animal sacred to him, he rose from the Oceanus, the river that surrounded all the earth, and drove his chariot across the sky vault, going from east to west.

Then he rested in the palace of the Hesperides, resting and letting the horses graze on the island of the Blessed.

In the evening he proceeded in the opposite direction, returning to his home that was located in the north. He used a golden boat, similar to a large bowl, forged by Hephaestus, which, sailing on the river Oceanus, brought him back to his destination along with the chariot and horses.

When he traveled on his golden chariot, pulled by four horses with golden manes, breathing fire from their nostrils, he wore a golden helmet covered with precious stones and gave off a light so dazzling that the human eye could not bear it.

As he passed, the land was covered with light and heat, and when he walked away, plowing through the ocean, night and darkness occurred.

With his eyes he could see exactly everything that happened on the ground, and so he watched all events, whether they concerned men or gods.

Precisely for this reason he was often invoked as a witness to oaths.

He had many children, seven by the Nymph Rodo, called Heliades. Legend has it that, in love with the nymph, he called the island of Rhodes by her name. Draining the water that covered it, he formed living creatures from its soil, the seven Heliades. Just then, in Rhodes a huge statue was dedicated to the god Helios, known to history as the "Colossus of Rhodes", one of the seven wonders of the world.

The islanders were peaceful and devoted to commerce but nevertheless were often attacked and conquered by other peoples. Once, they managed to defeat their Greek opponents who abandoned much of their military equipment on the island while fleeing. So the inhabitants of Rhodes decided to sell it and used the proceeds to build a large statue of the god Helios, as a sign of gratitude for the victory.

The statue was placed at the entrance of the port of the city and is said to have been 33 meters high, and it was bronze, with an internal reinforcement made of iron.

Some also say that it served as a beacon for ships entering the port.

We know exactly that the building was finished in 280 BC, but in 226 BC a violent earthquake broke the statue, which fell to the ground and was never rebuilt.

Then by Climene Helios had another son, Phaeton, whose name is linked to a sad story.

Phaeton, who in childhood had been brought up in Egypt, had always longed to be able to drive the chariot of the sun.

When he became older, one day decided to go to his father's palace, beyond the horizon, to submit his request. At first, Helios could not be moved, because driving the chariot required strength, skill and experience, and in his opinion, Phaeton was too young for such a task. But the son said and promised so much that eventually he persuaded his father to give him the chariot, but only for a day.

Helios made many recommendations about what to do and told him not to go too high nor too low, to follow the usual path, to hold the reins firmly, etc ...

When the dawn came, Phaeton began his trip on the chariot, but at a certain point, he drove the horses to an excessive speed and lost control. The sun came too close to ground, burning the vegetation, and turning the once fertile lands into deserts.

Then he walked away, and the earth cooled and the ice advanced.

Phaeton pleaded to his father, but he could not do anything to help him and watched the scene, shocked.

The god Zeus, aware of all those upheavals and angered by the damage done to the world, struck the young senseless man with lightning, causing him to fall into the river Eridanus (today's Po).

The sisters of Phaeton, who had followed everything that had been done while crying bitterly, were turned into poplar trees near the banks of the river so that they could always stay beside the beloved brother.

Analysis and Understanding

1) Who were the siblings of Helios?
2) What path did he complete each day? And every night?

3) What was he wearing when he traveled on his chariot?

4) On what island was the statue of the "colossus"?

5) What destroyed it?

6) What did Phaethon ask his father, when he became older?

7) Why did the father refuse at first?

8) What happened when the chariot of the sun came too close to the Earth?

9) What did Phaeton do? Where did he fall?

10) Into what were her sisters transformed?

Reworking and Writing

1) The ancients thought that the planet Earth was the center of the universe and that the Sun revolved around the Earth, as it would have seemed in their experience and to the human eye.

This theory is called "geocentric" or "Ptolemaic", after Ptolemy of Alexandria, of the second century AD. He perfected the ideas already expressed by Aristotle around 340 BC.

There were some ancient scholars who claimed instead that the Sun was at the center and the planets revolved around it. It was only in the 16th century A.D. that this theory was adopted and took the name Copernican, after the Polish astronomer, Copernicus, who published it in 1543.

Do a search on these two theories.

The Dioscuri Castor and Pollux

The name means "son of Zeus". They were twin brothers, sons of Zeus and Leda; one was called Castor and the other, Pollux.

Legend has it that Zeus turned into a swan in order to seduce Leda, and she produced two eggs: from one of them were born Pollux and Helen, from the other Castor and Clytemnestra.

However, these last two were the children of another man, Tindaro; therefore Pollux, son of Zeus, was immortal, while Castor, being the son of a mortal, was not.

Sometimes they were both also called Tindarids.

They were educated by the centaur Chiron.

The first excelled in boxing and was very intelligent; the second excelled in running and was a skilled tamer of horses.

They participated in many adventures: both took part in the famous expedition of Jason and the Argonauts, who went in search of the Golden Fleece in Colchis.

During the journey, the Argonauts, assailed by a violent storm, saw on the heads of the Dioscuri, whorls of flames, and immediately afterwards the fury of the storm subsided.

Since then the so-called St. Elmo's fire has been attributed to the two, and they have become the protectors of sailors.

They participated in the hunt against for the Calydonian boar, a huge beast that killed livestock and destroyed crops. The boar had been sent by the goddess Artemis to punish the king Eneo.

He had forgotten to offer sacrifices to her during the annual rites for the twelve Olympian gods.

Many heroes took part in the hunt and managed, thanks to the valuable contribution of the hero Meleager, to defeat the animal.

Then the Dioscuri freed their sister Elena, who had been abducted by Theseus, and they returned her to Sparta, their city.

They were represented in the form of two beautiful youths, always together, wrapped in a cape, often holding the reins of their horses and sometimes wearing Phrygian caps on their heads.

It was said that they walked fast even over the greatest distances, and often were seen to appear during or after battles to announce the victory of one side or another.

Their cult was widespread and made many sacrifices in their honor.

It is said that one day, guests at the wedding of two cousins, kidnapped their two brides, daughters of Leucippus. A struggle ensued in which Castor was killed by a rival, Ida, and had to descend into the underworld, while Pollux, only wounded by Lynceus, was taken up to heaven by his father Zeus.

Being so attached to his brother, he asked the god to be able to meet the beloved Castor, even if it meant giving up his immortality.

Then Zeus was so moved by so much brotherly love that he permitted them to stay together, stating that they would spend one day in the netherworld and one day on Olympus.

Then, as a reward, he turned them into a constellation and made them shine in the sky; they are still there, in the form of the constellation of Gemini.

Analysis and Understanding

1) What does the term "Dioscuri" mean and what were they called?
2) What did Zeus transform into to make love to Leda?
3) By whom were they educated?
4) In what type of deeds did they participate?
5) How were they portrayed?
6) Why did they appear during or after battles?
7) What did they do after having been invited to the weddings of cousins?
8) What happened to Castor?
9) What did Pollux ask Zeus?
10) Into which constellation were they transformed?

Reworking and Writing

1) Many mythological creatures were transformed into constellations, usually as a reward, or to commemorate an event; do a search on the mythological origin of the signs of the zodiac.

Aeolus, the God of the Winds

Aeolus was the son of the sea god Poseidon and Arne, and had from the god Zeus the charge of monitoring the Winds. He kept them stored in a cave on the island of Lipari, in the Aeolian archipelago (islands which he named), where his palace was.

The winds had caused several disasters, (which some say also included the separation of Sicily from the rest of the continent and the separation of Spain from Africa), so Zeus had decided to lock them up in jars and, on the advice of his wife Hera, he had entrusted them to Aeolus.

Aeolus had a vast knowledge of the art of navigation and astronomy, so he could adjust the favorable and unfavorable winds for sailors, as Hera, his patroness, commanded him.

He had twelve children, six boys and six girls, who lived happily with him and his wife on the island.

The most important winds were the four children of Astreo (the stars) and Eos (Aurora or Dawn). The first was Boreas, the North Wind, the most violent.

Once he transfomed himself into a horse because he became enamored of the mares of Dardano and sired twelve horses, swift as the wind.

Because of his remarkable power he was the bearer of storms and severe damage.

Zephyr, however, also called Phoen, blew from the west and was sweet and beneficial. He heralded spring and favored seed germination and the awakening of nature after winter.

Then there was Euro, also called Vulturno, blowing from the east. He brought both humidity and storms, and rain, dry and beautiful weather and sometimes drought.

The fourth was Austro (whom we call Sirocco), who blew from the south and brought the rain; so he was always depicted as wet. In some periods of the year, he made navigation difficult.

To these another four minor winds should be added: Libeccio, also known as African, from the south-west, with wings enveloped in fog and mist; Cecia, or Greek, the northeast wind, depicted as an old man with white hair with a serpent's tail and holding a plate of olives; to him hail was attributed. Then there was Apeliotes, also called Subsolano, from the south-east, depicted as a young man carrying ripe fruit in his hands; there was Schirone, the northwest wind, represented as a bearded old man with an urn full of water that at any moment could be turned onto the ground.

All the winds were represented in human form, with swollen cheeks in the act of blowing.

Among them and the clouds, Aeolus was represented with a crown and a royal sceptre in his hand.

The winds were considered real gods because their blowing announced the different seasons of the year and influenced the main economic activities of the time: agriculture, shipping and trade.

In Homer's Odyssey, it tells that Odysseus (Ulysses), a veteran of the Trojan war, landed on the island of Lipari and was received with great hospitality by Aeolus. The hero told his travel adventures to him.

In gratitude Aeolus gave him a skin bag which held the winds unfavorable for navigation, advising him not to open it.

Odysseus was careful for nine days and nine nights that the wineskin was not opened, staying awake all the time. On the tenth day, he could no longer remain vigilant and fell asleep. While he slept, his companions, believing that a skin so well guarded by the hero contained treasures, opened it, and so all the headwinds were freed. The ship was pushed off course; however, Odysseus managed to return to Aeolus to apologize for his disobedience, though unintentional, but he was sent off on bad terms.

The sea unleashed a terrible storm that destroyed all Odysseus's other ships, except the one he was on. An octagonal tower was built in Athens in the first century B.C., the so-called Tower of the Winds, where each side was dedicated to one of the eight winds.

Analysis and Understanding

1) Where did Aeolus live?
2) What disasters were the winds said to have caused?
3) Who advised Zeus to entrust the winds to Aeolus?
4) What were the names of the most important winds?
5) How many minor winds were there and what were they called?
6) Where was the so-called Tower of the Winds built?
7) What did Aeolus give Odysseus?
8) How many days did Odysseus manage to stay awake?
9) Who opened the bag containing the winds and why?
10) What happened after the release of the unfavorable winds?

Reworking and Writing

1) Draw the "wind rose", the figure representing the cardinal points and their derivations.

Draw the eight-point wind-rose. (There is also a type which has just four points, showing only the four cardinal points).

2) Do you know what wind power is? Today it is known that wind is one of the alternative sources of energy; renewable and clean. Do some research on the subject.

The Nine Muses

They were the goddesses that protected the arts. Their home was on Mount Helicon, in Boeotia, full of divine springs: the spring of Aganippe, the spring of Castalia and that of Hippocrene. This last one sprang from the soil of Mount Helicon after the winged horse Pegasus had struck the ground there with its hoof. People believed that the waters of the spring of Hippocrene gave inspiration to poets for their compositions.

They were daughters of the god Zeus and the nymph Mnemosyne, who in turn was the daughter of Uranus (the sky) and Gaea (the earth). Mnemosyne means "memory", and she was indeed the goddess who presided over memory. Their number was at first unknown, then tradition set it at nine, one for each of the major arts.The allocation of this or that artistic genre to each of them is not always agreed upon. They had numerous appellations that often referred to places where they were (for example Heliconias, Tespiadi, Citeriadi, Ligie, Lidie, Parnassidi, Partenidi, etc.)

They were employed by the god Phoebus, who was regarded as their master and who directed their chants. Often they intervened to enliven the banquets of the gods. Their first song was to mark the victory of the Olympian gods against the Titans, to celebrate the birth of a new order for the universe. They sang at the wedding of Peleus and Thetis and at those of Cadmus and Harmony too.

They often were represented crowned with violets, the sacred flower that indicated kingship and power, and with a sprig of laurel in their hands. They inspired singers and artists in general. Therefore, it was customary that artists invoked the protection and help of the Muses before attempting to compose their works, as if human capacity alone was not enough to call to mind what is worthy of being handed down.

They are also considered the ultimate expression of capacity of human knowledge, inspiration of the higher forms of spiritual life and intellectual faculties. They assured order, wisdom and harmony. An extended worship at cultural associations was dedicated to the Muses in Greece. They gave rise to the term "museum" to refer to the building which housed works inspired by them, and to the term "music" with all its derivatives. The poet Homer called Sappho, a sublime Greek poetess, "the tenth Muse".

Legend has it that one day the goddess Athena went to Mount Helicon, and began to chat with the Muses. At a certain point, there was a flutter of wings and they saw nine magpies perched on branches, uttering words of greeting and complaining of their fate. The goddess wondered what was happening and asked for an explanation from the Muses, who told what had happened. Shortly before, nine maidens, called Pierides after their father, Pierio of Pella, generated by Evippa, had climbed Mount Helicon to challenge the Muses to a singing contest. Whoever won would remain on Helicon, and the losers would be removed forever. The Muses at first did not want to accept the challenge, but then they agreed so as not to appear cowardly. Nymphs were chosen to decide who was going to win. They sat down on the stones around the area and listened to the whole contest.

In the end, the victory was given to the Muses, and it was a fair trial, because the nymphs had sworn on the rivers that they would be objective in judging. But the Pierides did not accept the verdict of the Nymphs and began to insult them. So Calliope, who was the protagonist of the contest and the victory, along with her companions, rebuked the Pierides, who not only dared to challenge them but now also were being so insolent.

The Pierides started laughing, but then dismayed, realized that their arms were becoming feathered wings, and their faces were turning into beaks. In fact, they were turning into magpies.

Even today magpies retain the habit of continually emitting hoarse sounds and cries.

There is also a legend that tells how the cicadas, before the arrival of the Muses, were men.

Taken with the pleasure of singing, they forgot even to eat and drink; so they died without realizing it.

Then the seed of the cicadas arose from them. The Muses granted them to gift of singing without eating, giving them the task of informing the Muses about what men would honor on earth.

Each Muse, as we said, presided over a particular aspect of art or science:

Calliope, "The one who has a beautiful voice," was the Muse of epic and lyric poetry. She was loved by Phoebus, with whom she had a son, Imène. He became the god of weddings and wedding songs. Some also say Orpheus, the divine singer, was her son. Calliope was depicted holding a stylus and writing tablets.

Clio was "the one that makes famous." She was the Muse of history, the one who sang the exploits of victory. She was depicted crowned with laurel, with a trumpet in one hand and a book or scroll in the other.

Erato, "The one who arouses desires", presided over erotic poetry (i.e., love) and over mime. She was depicted as a maiden crowned with myrtle and roses, who held in her left hand a lyre and in her right, a bow. Sometimes she was surrounded by doves.

Euterpe was "the one who rejoices." She was the Muse of music, lyric poetry and the flute. She was depicted crowned with flowers, playing the flute, which it is said she invented.

Melpomene was the "singer", the Muse of tragedy. She was loved by the river god Achelous, by whom some say she had the Sirens. She was represented crowned with vine leaves while holding a mask of tragic theater, or a scepter and a bloody dagger.

Polyhymnia, "full of hymns", was the Muse of rhetoric, the art of speaking well, and of sacred poetry; one that was dedicated to the gods and heroes. She was sometimes called "the one who does remember," taking a characteristic of her mother, Memnosyne, Memory, in fact. She was depicted with a crown of flowers or pearls, dressed in white, holding a scepter.

Talia: "the festive", the Muse of happy poetry, thus, comedy and satirical poetry. Legend has it that she was loved by Apollo and she gave him the Corybantes, priests of Cybele, who worshiped the goddess with wild dancing and parties. She is depicted as crowned with ivy, holding a mask and wearing boots to her knees.

Terpsichore, "the one who delights in dance", was the Muse of dance and choral lyrics, and was represented holding a lyre, the stringed musical instrument also called a cithara. She wore garlands of flowers around her head.

Urania, "the heavenly," whose name was derived from the Greek Ouranos, the Sky, presided over astronomy, geometry and astrology. She was represented crowned with stars, with a blue cape and holding up a globe, surrounded by mathematical tools.

Analysis and Understanding

1) Where did the nine Muses live?
2) Whose daughters were they? What does "Mnemosyne" mean?
3) Why did they have many names?
4) Who was considered their master?
5) Who was called the "tenth muse"?
6) Who served as referee in the match between the Muses and the Pierides?
7) How did the contest end and what did Calliope do?
8) What were the Pierides turned into?
9) What were the cicadas before, according to the legend?
10) Calliope was the inspiration for what kind of poetry?

Reworking and Writing

1) Define the meaning of the lyric and epic poetry.

2) Do a quick search on tragedy and comedy in ancient Greece.

3) It's strange that astronomy is connected to the arts such as music or poetry. Why do you think this happened?

Prometheus and the Gift of Fire

Prometheus was a Titan, son of the nymph Clymene and the Titan Eurymedon, or as others say, of the Titan Iapetus. His brothers were Epimethus, Atlas and Menoetius. We have already said how Atlas ended up, guilty of having participated in the struggle against the gods, he was forced to support upon his shoulders the vault of heaven; Menoetius then was killed by Zeus with a thunderbolt, as were other Titans. Instead Prometheus, whose name means "prescient", took the side of Zeus and the other gods of Olympus, and also convinced Epimetheus, "the seer after", to do the same.

They say that Prometheus created the human race by molding clay and giving it life, because he realized that of all the creatures, there was no ability to use the forces of nature, to create order among the animal species and understand the essence of things. He thought then to create man who could do this.

He had learned from the goddess Athena the arts and sciences, architecture, astronomy, mathematics, medicine, metallurgy, the art of navigation, etc., all things which he in turn, taught to mortals. Zeus was angered by this because he intended to destroy mankind and instead saw them become more and more experienced and powerful.

One day Prometheus went so far as to deceive the powerful chief of the gods: he was called as a referee in a discussion. The men did not know which part of a bull to sacrifice to the gods and which part to preserve for themselves. Then with the skin of the bull, he formed two bags, in one he set the flesh, hidden by the stomach, a barely edible and and very unappealing part, in the another he set bones covered by fat, which at that time was very much appreciated. Zeus was tricked and chose the bag with the bones and fat, but upon realizing it he punished Prometheus and the men by removing their fire.

Prometheus did not give in, and with the help of Athena, secretly entered the home of the gods, Olympus, and stole fire from the gods, hiding it in an iron rod, that he then brought it back to the men. Then Zeus, furious at the offense, ordered Hephaestus to tie the Titan to a mountain in the Caucasus and he inflicted a terrible punishment: a vulture (or an eagle, some say) every day was going to devour his liver, and this punishment never ended; it happened every day since during the night the liver grew back and the wounds healed.

Then, one day Prometheus revealed to him a prophecy that warned him about marrying Thetis; otherwise he would have a son who would dethrone him. Zeus, grateful, ordered Heracles to free the Titan, but he preferred to stay where he was, as a constant reminder of what he had done for mankind, and then Zeus turned him into a mountain, perhaps the old Ceraunius, today Mt. Elbrus, 5630 meters high, the highest peak of the Caucasus, which is among other things, an ancient volcano.

Analysis and Understanding

1) Who were the brothers of Prometheus?
2) What does the name "Prometheus" mean?
3) And the name "Epimetheus"?
4) According to the legend, how did Prometheus create the human race?
5) Which god did he deceive?
6) How did Zeus punish Prometheus and men?
7) What then did Prometheus do?
8) What punishment was he forced to endure for stealing fire from the gods?
9) Why then did Zeus order the release of the

Titan?

10) Into what was he changed?

Reworking and Writing

1) Even in other mythologies, as we have already seen, there is the presence of the formation of man from dust or from mud. In the Bible, we read (Genesis, 2:7) that the Lord God, having formed man from the dust of the earth, "breathed into his nostrils the breath of life and man became a living soul." What difference do you notice from the myth of Prometheus?

2) Why do you think Zeus punished Prometheus so cruelly?

Pandora

To punish men for the outrage of the theft of fire, Zeus decided to send among them a woman (obviously the king of the gods was sexist, if the woman was considered a punishment for mankind). He called Hephaestus, the blacksmith of the gods, and ordered him to make a woman. Hephaestus naturally obeyed and went to work. After a while he created the first woman, who was called Pandora. She received a gift from each of the gods (Pandora means "one who has all gifts"): she was beautiful, clever and persuasive in speaking, but also smart and a liar.

Athena had given her elegant clothes and a garland of flowers to adorn her head, and had taught her the art of weaving and embroidery. Aphrodite had given her great beauty. The Graces gave her some gold necklaces and other jewelry. Hermes gave her the ability to speak well and the art of persuasion, but also curiosity and we will see what happened because of this. Finally Zeus gave her a pot with a lid, in which he said that all the world's ills were enclosed.

He told her to take it with her everywhere but absolutely not to open it; otherwise, the evils would spread throughout the world, but closed inside there, they would not be able to bring harm to anyone.

When Pandora arrived on earth, Epimetheus was immediately seduced by her beauty. His brother Prometheus (remember that the name means "He who sees first, which provides") tried in vain to dissuade him from marrying the woman. Epimetheus, completely won over by her charms, would not listen to reason and married her.

Everything seemed to be going well. One day, however, Pandora, forgetting the recommendations of Zeus, out of curiosity, decided to raise only a little, the lid of the jar that she had been given, just to take a look inside and see what it really contained. Certainly she did not imagine what would happen because of her rash gesture: just lifting the lid, Old Age, Fatigue, Illness, Vice, Passion and all the other troubles rushed out, spreading across the world and began to plague mortals.

Only Hope didn't leave and remained trapped in the jar because Zeus had a little pity for mankind and granted to men that at least hope remained. That is always the last thing that remains, to be able to endure life and its worries.

Analysis and Understanding

1) Why did Zeus decide to send a woman amongst men?
2) Who put him in charge of making her?
3) What was she called, and what does it mean?
4) What gift did Hermes give her? And what about Zeus?
5) Who fell in love with her immediately, as soon as she came to earth?
6) Who tried to convince Epimetheus to hold back from his plan?
7) What did Pandora do one day, out of curiosity?
8) What happened then?
9) Who remained in the jar instead?
10) Why did hope remain, enclosed in the jar?

Reworking and Writing

1) The names Prometheus and Epimetheus mean opposite things; explain what these names mean and how they befit the behavior displayed by the two brothers on this occasion.

2) Even today there is a saying: "Hope is the last to die". Discuss its meaning with examples from your own experience.

Deucalion and Pyrrha

Men had become evil and corrupt, then Zeus decided to punish them, causing a terrible flood on earth.

Deucalion, king of Phthia, was warned by his father, the Titan Prometheus, what would happen, so he built an ark, loaded it with food and climbed in with his wife Pyrrha. In fact, after a while, as Prometheus had predicted, an incessant rain began. It swelled rivers and raised the sea level until the whole earth was covered by water and all mortals perished. Only Deucalion and Pyrrha were saved, in their ark, floating on the water with no clear direction.

When the fury of the elements subsided, the ark came to rest on Mount Parnassus in Greece. Then the two disembarked and went to pray at the shrine of Themis, Justice. They offered sacrifices to Zeus and asked him to revive mankind.

Zeus then, convinced by the prayers of the two, sent Hermes, messenger of the gods, to them, who told them that anything they asked for they would get. At that time, the goddess Themis in person appeared and ordered them to bow their heads, cover themselves with a veil and throw the bones of their mother behind them.

The two looked stunned, not knowing what to do and how to interpret these strange words. Then, at last, they understood that the bones were nothing but stones, sons of mother earth. Then they obeyed and threw the stones that little by little they had gathered. From the stones thrown by Deucalion were born men; from those cast by Pyrrha instead, were born women. This way humankind repopulated the earth.

The legend also says that then from Deucalion, Hellen, the ancestor of all the Greeks, was born.

Analysis and Understanding

1) Why did Zeus decide to punish men?
2) Who warned Deucalion?
3) What did he do then?
4) What happened after he built an ark?
5) Where did the ark end up when the flood ended?
6) Which shrine did Deucalion and Pyrrha go to?

7) What did they ask Zeus?

8) What did the goddess Themis order them to do?

9) Who was born from the stones they threw?

10)   Who was the ancestor of all the Greeks?

Reworking and Writing

1) The story of the great flood is present in the traditions of many peoples very distant from each other: it is talked about in the Bible, with the famous episode of Noah and the ark: in Mesopotamia, in Indian, Chinese, and ancient Mexican texts.

We cannot know whether the events described are a single catastrophe which affected the entire globe, or whether they are different incidents which occurred at different times, more limited in scope.

Below there is the Biblical passage which speaks of the flood.

After reading it carefully, write down the differences that you can find between it and the myth of Deucalion and Pyrrha.

Preparation of the Flood (Genesis 6, 13 -22)

Then God said to Noah: " The end of all flesh has come before Me, for the land, because of them, is filled with violence; behold, I will destroy them with the earth. Make yourself an ark of gopher wood; make compartments in the ark, and cover it inside and outside with pitch. That's how you do it:

the ark shall be three hundred cubits long, fifty wide and thirty high. You shall make a roof for it, leaving below the roof an opening one cubit hih all around and set the door of the ark in its side. You shall make it with lower, middle and upper decks.

Behold, I bring a flood of waters upon the earth, to destroy from under heaven all flesh, wherein is the breath of life; everything that is on earth shall perish. But I will establish my covenant with you. Come into the ark, you and your sons with you, your wife and your sons' wives. Of every living thing of all flesh, you shall bring into the ark two of every sort, to keep them alive with you; they shall be male and female. Of the birds after their kind, and of cattle after their kind, of every creeping thing of the earth after its kind, two of every kind will come to you, to keep them alive. And you shall take for yourself of all food that is eaten, and you shall gather it to yourself; and it shall be food for you and for them." Noah did everything as God commanded him, so he did he.

Preparation of the Flood (Genesis 7: 1-9)

The Lord then said to Noah, "Go into the ark, you and your whole family, because I have found you righteous in this generation. Take with you seven pairs of every kind of clean animal, a male and his mate, and one pair of every kind of unclean animal, a male and his mate, and also seven pairs of every kind of bird, male and female, to keep their various kinds alive over all the earth. Seven days from now

I will send rain on the earth for forty days and forty nights, and I will wipe from the face of the earth every living creature I have made." And Noah did all that the Lord commanded him. Noah was six hundred years old when the flood of waters came on the earth. And Noah and his sons and his wife and his sons' wives entered the ark to escape the waters of the flood. Pairs of clean and unclean animals, of birds and of all creatures that move along the ground, male and female, came with Noah into the ark, as God had commanded Noah.

The Flood (Genesis 7: 17-24)

For forty days the flood was on the earth and as the waters increased, they lifted the ark high above the earth. The waters rose and increased greatly on the earth, and the ark floated on the water. The waters rose up more and more over the earth; and all the high mountains that were under the whole sky were covered. The waters rose and covered the mountains to a depth of more than fifteen cubits. And every living thing that moved on the earth perished, birds, livestock, wild animals, all the creatures that swarm on the earth, and all mankind. Every creature that had the breath of life in its nostrils, all that was on dry land, died. So every being that was on earth was exterminated with men, animals, reptiles and birds of the air: and they were destroyed from the earth and Noah only remained and those who were with him in the ark.

And the waters prevailed upon the earth a hundred and fifty days.

The Lowering of the Water (Genesis 8: 1-14)

But God remembered Noah, and all the wild animals and the livestock that were with him in the ark. God sent a wind over the earth and the waters receded. The fountains of the deep and the floodgates of heaven were closed, and the rain from heaven had stopped falling from the sky; the water receded steadily from the ground. At the end of the hundred and fifty days the water decreased. Then the ark rested in the seventh month, the seventeenth day of the month, on the mountains of Ararat. The water decreased gradually until the tenth month. In the tenth month, on the first day of the month, the tops of the mountains were seen. After forty days Noah opened the window of the ark which he had made and he sent out a raven, which kept going to and fro until the waters had dried up from the earth. Then he sent out a dove to see if the waters were abated from the surface of the ground. But the dove found no resting place for the sole of its foot, and it returned into the ark to him, for the waters were on the face of the whole earth. He reached out his hand and took the dove and brought it back with him into the ark. He waited yet another seven days and again he sent the dove out from the ark, and the dove came to him in the evening, and behold, in its mouth there was an olive branch. Noah knew that the waters had receded from the earth. He waited another seven days, and sent forth the dove; it did not return to him anymore. And it came to pass in the six hundred and first year, in the first month, the first day of the month, that the waters were dried up from the earth; Noah removed the covering of the ark and saw that the face of the ground was dry. In the second month, on the twenty-seventh day of the month, the earth was dry.

The Output from the Ark (Genesis 8: 15-20)

God commanded Noah: "Go out, you and your wife, and your sons and your sons' wives with you. Bring out with you all the animals of each species that you have with you, birds and cattle and every living creatures that creeps on the earth, so they can breed on earth, and be fruitful and multiply upon it." So Noah went out with his sons, his wife and his sons' wives. All the animals and all the cattle and all the birds and all the creatures that move along the ground according to their kinds, came out of the ark. Then Noah built an altar to the Lord and, taking some of each sort of clean animals and clean bird, and he made burnt offerings on it.

Cadmus and the Dragon's Teeth

Cadmus was the son of the Phoenician king Agenor and brother of Europa. She had been kidnapped by the god Zeus transformed into a bull. The father Agenor then sent Cadmus, with his brothers Cilice and Phoenix, to search for her, but when he went to the oracle of Delphi, Cadmus was advised to stop the search, since he was intended to be the founder of a great city.

He would be led by a cow with a crescent imprinted on its hide, and where the animal stopped, there he would have to build the city.

So it was, when the animal fell to the ground, exhausted, Cadmus knew that there he had to stop.

He sent some comrades to draw water for the sacrifice of good wishes from a nearby spring.

They did not return because the spring had been placed under the supervision of a dragon that lived in a nearby cave, and had killed them.

Then, holding only a stone, Cadmus alone fought and killed the monstrous snake.

Then the goddess Athena appeared. She invited him to sow the dragon's teeth; from those a group of armed warriors, very threatening, were born.

Then Cadmus threw stones between them, and believing that they had been struck by their comrades, they accused each other. They fought fiercely until only five survived.

They helped Cadmus to found the city of Thebes in Boeotia, "the country's cow", and were the ancestors of the Thebans.

Then Cadmus married the beautiful Harmony. Their wedding was a memorable feast attended by all the gods.

Legend has it that the two then emigrated to the land of the Illyrians. After having defeated them, Cadmus became their king.

The legend also says that Cadmus and Harmony were transformed into snakes, and after they died they were welcomed into the Elysian Fields, the place where the deceased who were well-liked by the gods lived.

Among other things, it's said that Cadmus brought the letters of the Phoenician alphabet to Greece.

Analysis and Understanding

1) Whose brother was Cadmus?
2) Who advised him to stop searching for Europa and why?
3) What animal would guide him?
4) At what point did Cadmus stop?
5) Why did he send his comrades to fetch water?
6) Who was guarding the spring?
7) Which goddess advised him to sow the dragon's teeth?
8) What was born from the teeth?
9) What does the term "Beotia" mean? Which town did Cadmus found?

10) Who then married Cadmus? Where did they go after their deaths?

Reworking and Writing

1) From history, we know that the Phoenicians, experienced sailors and traders, invented their own alphabet for business purposes. The Greek alphabet derived from this, and from that the Latin alphabet. Do a search on the subject.

2) Find tales about Europa, the sister of Cadmus, who gave her name to the entire continent.

Daedalus and Icarus

Daedalus was a great architect, sculptor, and inventor, who lived on Crete.

One day he committed a heinous crime. Since his nephew Talos, who was his apprentice, was becoming more skilled than he, using an excuse, he brought him to the roof of a temple and, blinded by jealousy, he pushed him down. The legend says that Talos was transformed into a partridge by the gods.

Daedalus fled to Crete, where King Minos welcomed him with pleasure, knowing his mastery. In fact, he built the famous labyrinth for Minos, beneath the palace of Knossos, where the Minotaur, a half-man, half-bull monster, was imprisoned.

The maze was an intricate path that once inside, prevented anyone from getting out. But Daedalus helped Theseus to escape after the hero had killed the Minotaur, by giving a thread to Ariadne, that she then gave to Theseus. This allowed the hero to find the exit.

For this, Minos locked up Daedalus and his son Icarus, to punish them for the help provided to Theseus. But the clever inventor did not give in and devised a means to regain freedom.

He built a pair of wings for his son and a pair for himself, with bird feathers and wax, and they both put them on. He recommended, however, to his son, the first to fly, to be careful and not to go too high, otherwise the sun would melt the wax, and not to fly too, otherwise the sea water would dampen feathers. But the boy, once up, excited by flight, pointed himself upward.

The heat of the sun softened the wax that held the feathers and it finally broke up. The unfortunate young man fell into the sea and was swallowed by the waves. When the father turned to see where he was, he was not there, but he saw only a few feathers floating. Full of pain, he waited for the body to resurface, then buried it on a nearby island. For this reason, this part of the Aegean Sea is called the Icarian Sea.

And legend has it that a partridge surveyed the scene squealing with joy: it was the soul of Talos, finally avenged.

It is said that Daedalus landed in Cuma in Campania, and from there he went first to Sicily, then to Sardinia, leaving traces everywhere of big and beautiful buildings, that were called "Daedalic" after him.

Analysis and Understanding

1) What animal was Talo turned into?
2) Where did Daedalus flee?
3) What did he build for Minos?
4) Who was locked up in the Labyrinth?
5) Why did Minos punish Daedalus by enclosing him in the Labyrinth?
6) Who was locked up with him?
7) What did Daedalus think of doing to get out?
8) Did Icarus follow the recommendations of his father?
9) What happened when the sun melted the wax?
10) What animal surveyed the scene of the burial, and who was in reality?

Reworking and Writing

1) The construction style, "Daedalic," is also known as "megalithic," meaning, "large stones." In Italy, this style is found primarily on Sardinia. Do research on the subject.

2) Draw a dolmen, the typical Sardinian megalithic construction.

Theseus and the Minotaur

Theseus, considered the founder of Athens, was its king. He was also the initiator of the most famous Athenian traditions. He performed many heroic deeds, such as killing monsters and robbers who infested the area, but his most famous deed is the killing of the Minotaur.

King Minos of Crete, having won the war against Athens, had imposed a heavy toll: every year (or every nine years, according to another version of the myth), seven boys and seven girls were to be sent to Crete to be fed to the Minotaur, the fierce monster with the body of man and the head of a bull who lived locked up in the labyrinth (built by Daedalus, see the previous story).

The brave Theseus, son of King Aegeus, volunteered to participate in the third expedition, with the intention of killing the monster. He promised his father that if he won, he would return with white sails hoisted on his ship, but if the mission had not been successful, instead there would be black sails, and he left.

When he arrived on Crete, the daughter of King Minos, Ariadne, fell in love with him, and helped him to get out of the maze by giving him the famous "Ariadne's Thread": after entering the maze and having killed the monster with the strength of his own hand, indeed, Theseus was able to find the exit by reversing the ball of thread that he had unrolled upon entering.

Then he set off in the direction of Athens with the children, safe and sound, and with Ariadne, whom he had promised to marry. Except that things did not go entirely smoothly.

He stopped on the island of Naxos. While Ariadne rested on the island, the hero returned to the ship. But a violent storm turned the ship away from the island and what's more, once the storm was over, Theseus forgot all about the unfortunate Ariadne. Some say he was encouraged to do so by Dionysus, the god of wine; Theseus probably got drunk. The girl, awoke and seeing she had been abandoned, cried with despair and cursed her ungrateful lover. She will later be saved by Dionysus, who will welcome her into his ranks.

Meanwhile Theseus sailed towards Athens, but also forgot to change the sails, and to hoist the white ones (he had a very poor memory, then!), as a sign of the success of the enterprise.

His father Aegeus, seeing the black sails from afar and believing that his son was dead, threw himself into the waters of the sea below in a act of despair. Since then the sea surrounding the Greece has taken his name, Aegean, which it is called today.

After becoming king of Athens and bringing development and glory to the city, Theseus accomplished still more deeds: he may have gone with Heracles in the expedition against the Amazons; some say that he followed Jason and the Argonauts in the quest for the Golden Fleece; others that he even descended into Tartarus to kidnap the goddess Persephone.

Even his death is shrouded in mystery; it is said that he was killed by a trap by Lycomedes, king of Skyros when he took refuge on the island after his throne was usurped.

Analysis and Understanding

1) What is the most famous deed of Theseus?
2) What was the tax imposed by Minos on the city of Athens?
3) Who was the Minotaur?
4) What did Theseus promise to his father, Aegeus?
5) Who was Ariadne and what did she give to Theseus?
6) On which island did he leave her during the return trip?
7) Who saved Ariadne?
8) What did Theseus forget to do?

9) What did his father, Aegeus, do then? Why?

10) Of which city did Theseus become king?

Reworking and Writing

1) Ariadne and Dionysus (with the Latin name of Bacchus) appear in a famous poem by Lorenzo de' Medici, the Magnificent (Florence, 1449-1492), which is titled "The Triumph of Bacchus and Ariadne". We have already spoken of this as regards Dionysus. Search for it with the teacher's help, and find the passage where he speaks of Ariadne.

2) Do a search on the different names that the Mediterranean has in different regions, including Italy.

Orpheus and Eurydice

Orpheus was a legendary singer, the son of the king of Thrace, Eagro, and the Muse Calliope. He had received as a gift from the god Phoebus, a lyre, the stringed musical instrument which is also called the cithara. The Muses taught him to use it.

He was so good that when he played everything and everyone stopped, enchanted by that sweet sound; even the wild beasts were pacified; even trees and rocks moved to follow him and his music. His wife was the beautiful Eurydice.

One sad day, however, in a valley at Tempe, in Thrace, while trying to escape the evil Aristeo chasing her, Eurydice tripped over a snake which bit her, causing her to die. Orpheus wept and despaired, then decided to carry out an almost impossible task, that is, go down to the underworld to bring back his wife.

So he went down into Tartarus using a secret passage and, once he arrived in the Underworld, there he also charmed everyone with his music: the dog Cerberus, Charon, the boatman, the three judges of the dead, etc. Even the damned had their suffering stopped for a bit. The same Hades, lord of the Underworld, was enchanted and his heart was touched by the sweet melodies of Orpheus.

Hades consented easily that Euridice could return to earth, but he placed only one condition in regards to her return to the living world: Orpheus could not turn around to look at her until she had reached the light of day. The two then began the journey back.

Eurydice followed enchanted by the music of her husband and after a while reached the top of the abyss; but Orpheus, failing in his covenant with Hades, and unable to restrain himself, turned too soon to look at Eurydice. As soon as he did it, the poor woman was lost forever. She was again swallowed up by the dark underworld and could not return to earth.

Orpheus pleaded in vain to Charon, the boatman of Hades, to return, trying to save Eurydice again.

He was forced to return alone to the earth, where he began to gather around him, crowds of young people, teaching them to worship the god Phoebus with mystery rites. Precisely for this reason, the Maenads, the priestesses of Dionysus, killed him because he had made sacrifices to their god.

Legend has it that Zeus, moved by the the singer's death, took him to the sky, making him the constellation Lyra.

Analysis and Understanding

1) From whom did Orpheus receive the lyre?
2) Who had taught him to use it?
3) What happened when he played?
4) Who was his wife?
5) How did Eurydice die?
6) What did Orpheus then decide?
7) In the underworld, who was enchanted by his music?
8) What condition did Hades pose to return Eurydice to earth?
9) Why did Orpheus turn?
10) What happened then?

Reworking and Writing

1) Orpheus turned not merely out of curiosity, but for the great love that bound him to Eurydice; explain in your own words if you can figure this out, or if it was completely wrong.

2) Do a search on Hades, the dark underworld of the ancient Greeks.

3) Find images of the constellation Lyra and draw it in your notebook.

Perseus and Medusa

Perseus was the son of Zeus and Danae.
Legend has it that the king Acrisius, father of Danae, had learned from an oracle that a son of Danae would depose him. So when Perseus was born, he locked him with his mother in wooden chest and threw it into the sea.
But the waves brought the chest to an island of the Cyclades, where King Polydectes received them graciously, hosting them in his court.
When Perseus become an adult, the king ordered him to bring him the head of Medusa, who was one of the three Gorgons and was the only one of them who was mortal.

These three female monsters, with boar tusks instead of teeth and snakes instead of hair, had the power to turn into stone anyone who looked at them.

The hero succeeded with the help of Athena and Hermes.

He went first to the Nymphs, who gave him winged sandals, a helmet of invisibility and a bag in which to store the head of Medusa.

Athena instead gave him a shield of ivory, polished like a mirror, advising him not to look directly at the Gorgon, but only at her reflection.

Hermes gave him a sharp sickle.

The boy left and arrived in the land of the Hyperboreans, the legendary people of the North, where he found the three Gorgons sleeping.

Using the shield as a mirror, he managed to decapitate Medusa, from whose blood the winged horse Pegasus and the warrior Crisaore were born.

Using the helmet of invisibility, Perseus managed to escape, but another adventure was waiting for him.

On the return trip, while passing along the coast, the hero saw a girl chained to a rock and immediately fell in love with her.

She was Andromeda, who was offered as a sacrifice to appease the wrath of the Nereids, the sea goddesses, offended by Andromeda's mother, Cassiopeia.

Cassiopeia had boasted that both she and her daughter were more beautiful than the sea goddesses.

They then decided that Andromeda had to be fed to a sea monster to make amends for the offense they had received.

Thus, the poor girl had been tied to a rock until the monster could arrive to devour her.

When the monster was near the cliff, Perseus, using the head of Medusa turned the monster into stone and rescued the girl. After marrying her, he returned to his homeland with her.

The legend ends with the punishment of King Acrisius. During the games to which he had been invited, Perseus, while throwing a disc, whether because of the wind or perhaps the will of the gods, accidentally struck Acrisius, who died.

Next, Perseus, who was Acrisius's grandson, became king of Tiryns and dedicated Medusa's head to Athena as thanks for helping him.

The goddess put the head in the center of her shield, as she has always been depicted.

Analysis and Understanding

1) Whose son was Perseus?
2) What did a legend say?
3) What did Acrisius, father of Danae, then do?
4) Where did the chest stop?
5) What did King Polydectes order to Perseus?

6) What did Athena advise Perseus, and what did she give him?
7) What was born from Medusa's blood?
8) Why was Andromeda to be sacrificed?
9) What did Perseus do to free Andromeda?
10) To whom did he dedicate the head of Medusa?

Reworking and Writing

1) The wooden chest in which Perseus and his mother Danae are locked reminds us of the basket entrusted to the waters of the Tiber where Romulus and Remus were placed. Do a search on the subject.

2) Compose a dialogue between Andromeda, bound to the rock, and Perseus, who decides to free her.

3) Draw Athena's shield with the head of Medusa.

Bellerophon and the Chimera

Bellerophon, having been guilty of grave offenses, left his city, Corinth, and asked for hospitality from Preto, king of Tiryns.

King Preto's wife had fallen in love with Bellerophon and had been rejected since he did not want to betray the young king's hospitality; so she unjustly accused him of trying to seduce her. Preto did not want to kill him because he was his guest and the guest was considered sacred, so he sent him to Iobates, the king of Lycia.

Even Iobates wouldn't kill him directly, so as not to renege on the sacred duties of hospitality, thus, he commissioned a very difficult task: to kill the Chimera, a monster that had a lion's head, a goat's body, a serpent's tail and fiery breath.

Before leaving for the arduous adventure, Bellerophon captured the winged horse Pegasus (which had been born from the blood of Medusa, the monster killed by Perseus) that lived on Mount Helicon. With the help of the goddess Athena, he was able to tame and harness it, then flying with it over the Chimera, surprised it, striking the monster with countless arrows. He then threw a block of lead into its jaws, which then melted from the heat of its breath, suffocating it.

He returned to King Iobates, but instead of receiving the honors for the victory, that he thought deserved, he was forced to leave again, because the king gave him another dangerous assignment. He had to defeat the Amazons and their allies, the people of Solìmi. With the help of Pegasus, which allowed him to fly over the enemy at a height where he could not be hit, Bellerophon was able to defeat even the Amazons and their allies.

Upon returning, Iobates deployed his army against him and decided to fight and kill him. But Bellerophon prayed to the god Poseidon, to overflow the river Xanthus, which flooded the plain and scared away the enemy. King Iobates, understanding that the young man was protected by the gods, told him of the charges against him received by Preto and demanded an explanation. Bellerophon told him the truth, and the king believed him. Iobates, to be forgiven, and as a reward for the value shown in the deeds that he had given him, gave him his daughter in marriage and appointed him heir to the throne. But the story does not end here.

The hero could have spent the rest of his days in peace and prosperity, but instead he was driven by an inordinate ambition to reach Olympus, riding his winged horse, to become part of the circle of the gods. But Zeus could not tolerate this insult, so he sent a gadfly that stung Pegasus under the tail. The winged horse then bolted and unseated the rider, who fell to the ground, injured and disappointed. Bellerophon was forced to wander alone on the earth, blind and crippled, far from busy roads, until the end of his days, because he had dared to challenge the gods.

Pegasus instead continued his run to Olympus, where Zeus received it and put it at his service, giving him the task of carrying the thunderbolts forged by the Cyclopes. These, as we know, were used by the king of the gods to frighten or punish men and gods.

Analysis and Understanding

1) Why did Bellerophon leave the town?
2) Why didn't Preto want to kill him?
3) What was the Chimera?
4) Before leaving on his task, what did Bellerophon do?
5) How did he kill the Chimera?
6) What new task did he face?
7) What god helped the hero to make the river Xanthus overflow?
8) Why did Bellerophon try to get to Olympus?
9) What did Zeus do then?
10) What task was entrusted by Zeus to Pegasus?

Reworking and Writing

1) Research the representations of the Chimera (paintings, statues, mosaics) made at any time, e.g., the famous Chimera of Arezzo, a statue of Etruscan manufacture of 5th or 6th century BC. Then try to draw it.

2) The term "chimera" has taken on another meaning. Find it in the vocabulary.

3) Explain in your words why Bellerophon was punished by Zeus, and whether or not he deserved the punishment that was imposed.

Tantalus

Tantalus was the son of Zeus and Titaness Pluto (Wealth). He ruled over vast territories and was very rich. He had been admitted to the table of the gods and, by listening to their speeches, he had become immortal.

He did not return the favor that the gods had shown him and in time became proud and went so far as to perform nefarious deeds. Indeed, he dared to steal nectar and ambrosia, the favorite foods of the gods, to give them to his mortal friends and to his subjects. He even dared to divulge the secrets that he had heard during the banquets of the gods.

Once, he stole a gold mastiff belonging to Hephaestus, the god of metalworking, and hid it. When the gods asked if he knew anything about the theft, Tantalus swore that he had never seen it, nor had he ever heard of it; but that was not enough. He went so far as to put in doubt the omniscience of the gods and wanted to test them. He devised a hideous plan: he killed his son Pelops, had him cooked, and served him during a banquet to which he invited the Olympian gods. The gods, however, gave evidence of being truly omniscient, because they knew what Tantalus had done. None of them touched the dish.

Only Demeter, lost in thought and saddened by the problem of the disappearance of her daughter

Persephone, had eaten a piece of the shoulder of the child. Hermes, however, picked up the various parts of the unfortunate boy, welded them together and brought him back to life. Then Zeus ordered Hephaestus to replace the missing piece with an ivory shoulder. Pelops emerged safe and sound from that adventure. He was so handsome that the sea god Poseidon took him to Olympus and made him his butler.

The gods were of course horrified by the action of Tantalus, and they decided to punish him harshly: they sent him to Tartarus, the dark underworld, where he was sentenced to undergo the famous "the torture of Tantalus": immersed in water up to his throat and tied to a tree fruit, he was unable to drink and to eat. Every time he bent down to drink, the water level went down, and every time he tried to collect the fruits, they moved out of his reach, driven upward by a wind that suddenly began to blow. He was then forced to suffer hunger and thirst for eternity.

Even today one says "suffer the torment of Tantalus" to denote the suffering of those who believe they have at hand something that they crave, but instead it escapes continuously.

Analysis and Understanding

1) Whose son was Tantalus?

2) What did he dare steal from the gods?

3) What did he steal from Hephaestus, and how did he behave when he was asked if he knew anything about this?

4) Of what did he doubt?

5) Which tremendous plan did he think up?

6) How did the gods become aware of what Tantalus had done?

7) Who picked up the pieces of Pelops and made him come back to life?

8) Who built an ivory shoulder for him?

9) What assignment did Pelops have on Olympus?

10) What punishment did the gods inflict on Tantalus?

Reworking and Writing

1) The legend says that Pelops then founded the city of Enete in the Turkish region of Paphlagonia. The names of the Italian region of Veneto region and of Venice would derive just from Enete. Indeed, it is said that some people of that region joined the Trojans led by Antenor, and, leaving from Turkey after the Trojan War, they arrived in the North-East of Italy. Do a search on the subject.

2) The punishment inflicted on Tantalus is definitely very hard, but do you think it was deserved? Express your opinions about it.

3) Give an example, taken from your daily experience, of " the torture of Tantalus ".

Pelops and Hippodamia

We have already met the character of Pelops in the myth that tells of his father Tantalus, the horrendous crime by which he was stained, for which he was severely punished by the gods, and the resurrection of Pelops.

Once he grew up, legend has it that Pelops left him homeland, which some say was Phrygia, others Lydia, anyway always in Asia Minor, and arrived in Greece, at the court of King Oenomaus of Pisa (the ancient town of Elide), who was the son of god Ares.

He had a daughter, the beautiful Hippodamia, whom he did not want to marry anyone because an oracle had predicted that he would die because of his future son-in-law. To prevent the wedding, he had proposed a bet: whoever would have his daughter's hand would have to defeat him in a chariot race along a course that went from his palace to the altar of Poseidon on the Isthmus of Corinth. If the suitor won, he would marry Hippodamia, but if he lost he would be killed by Oenomaus.

The king was sure to win because the chariot he rode on, equipped with mares as fast as the wind, had been given to him by his father, the god Ares. The charioteer, that is, who was driving the horses, was Myrtilus, son of the god Hermes, and the most experienced of all.

Oenomaus also required that Hippodamia also rode on the rival's chariot, so that the suitor, distracted by the girl's beauty, would lose focus and lose the race. He was so confident of winning that gave an advantage to the opponent: Oenomaus had him go first, while he lingered, making sacrifices to the gods, and only when the ritual was over did he begin to run after him. Despite this advantage, however, all the opponents were defeated. The king had them killed with a spear. He had their heads cut off and hung them in his palace as macabre trophies.

By now thirteen suitors had already been beaten and killed when Pelops appeared at the palace to challenge Oenomaus. He was equipped with a light chariot and fast mares, that the god Poseidon had given him. The beautiful Hippodamia immediately fell in love with the young man, and persuaded the charioteer Myrtilus to tamper with her father's chariot, replacing some spokes with wax, so he lost the bet. Others say it was Pelops, frightened by the scene of severed heads, that persuaded Myrtilus out of fear of losing the bet.

However, during the race, Oenomaus's chariot shattered to pieces. The king became entangled in the horse's reins and fell wounded to the ground. Before dying, having realized that he had been tricked, he cursed Myrtilus and wished that he be killed by the same Pelops. The curse came true: after the incident the three (Pelops, Hippodamia, and Myrtilus) fled far from the town, but Pelops did not keep the promise of reward that he agreed on with Myrtilus.

As a result, a dispute arose between the two young men, which ended with the killing of Myrtilus, who plunged into the sea from a rock that was located at the tip of the Greek peninsula of Euboea, and which took the name of Mirtoo.

Myrtilus's father, the god Hermes, who had heard the last words of his son, gave him accommodation for eternity in the starry sky, transforming him into the constellation of Auriga (the Charioteer).

In fact, the children and grandchildren of Pelops (Atreus, Thyestes, Agamemnon) met a tragic end. Pelops became king and became very rich, but his children never knew peace, although he had tried to make peace with Zeus by establishing the Olympic Games.

The legend says that it was Pelops who first founded them, then these games fell into disuse, but they were revived by the hero Heracles, in Pelops's memory and honor.

Analysis and Understanding

1) Whose son was Pelops?
2) To which king did he go, once he became an adult?
3) Who was Hippodamia?
4) Why did Oenomaus wish to prevent his daughter from marrying?
5) What happened to those who lost the race?
6) How many suitors had been killed before Pelops arrived at the palace?
7) Who was Myrtilus?
8) Who won the race and why?
9) Who killed Myrtilus and into what was he transformed after death?
10) Why did the descendants of Pelops never have peace?

Reworking and Writing

1) This legend also tells of the institution of the first Olympics. These athletic games were held at Olympia, in Elis, every four years, and athletes from all over Greece gathered there.

The winners were rewarded with only a crown of wild olive branches, but the glory of the athlete who won was immense.

History tells us that the first Olympiad was held in the year 776 B.C., an important date because Greeks counted the years from it.

Do a search on the subject, with reference to the resumption of the Olympic Games in modern times, by the Baron de Coubertin.

2) The motto of the Olympics re-established by Baron de Coubertin in 1896 in Athens, is the following: " The important thing is participating, not winning." Do you think that today this idea still has value, or is it often overshadowed? Express your thoughts on the subject.

Orion the Hunter

Orion was the best hunter of his day and the most beautiful of mortals. He had been blinded by King Enopione for reasons of jealousy, but Eos, the Dawn, fell in love with him and therefore his brother Helios, the Sun, restored his sight.
Orion, seeking revenge on Enopione, arrived on the island of Crete, and there he met Artemis, the goddess of hunting, who dissuaded him from thoughts of revenge and invited him to hunt with her.
But the god Phoebus, brother of Artemis, fearing that his sister had fallen victim to the charms of the handsome hunter, went to seek help from Mother Earth, who sent a poisonous scorpion after Orion.
The arrows and the sword with which Orion defended himself were of no avail, the scorpion

didn't give any sign of retreat, and indeed assailed him constantly, showing not a sign of vulnerability. Therefore, he decided to escape by jumping into the sea and swimming away in a hurry.

But Phoebus acted deceitfully: he showed his sister a point in the distance out to sea, saying it was the head of Candaone, a wicked man who had committed many crimes and challenged the goddess to hit him with her arrows.

Artemis, unaware of the truth, did so and struck the unfortunate man.

Then, when she swam out to reach him, she realized her horrible mistake, and desperate and weeping, begged Asclepius to return her beloved to life.

Asclepius would have answered, but Zeus struck him with a thunderbolt so he could not bring his work to completion.

For Artemis there was then nothing left but to take Orion into the sky and turn him into a constellation, followed for eternity by Scorpio.

Then the goddess placed at his feet his favorite hunting dogs, Canis Major and Canis Minor.

Analysis and Understanding

1) Why was Orion blinded by Enopione?
2) Who gave him back his sight and why?
3) Where did he go looking for Enopione, and whom did he meet there?

4) What was it that Phoebus feared?
5) What animal did Mother Earth send to confront Orion?
6) What did Orion do at the end?
7) Why did Artemis hit Orion with her arrows?
8) To whom did she beg to return her beloved to life?
9) Why could Asclepius not help her?
10)   What did Artemis do then?

Reworking and Writing

1) Do a search on the constellations of Orion, Scorpio, Canis Major and Canis Minor, then draw them in the notebook.

2) If in ancient times hunting was a way to get food, today it has become just a sport. Are you in favor of hunting or not? Express your personal views on the subject.

Jason and the Quest for the Golden Fleece

Jason was the legitimate heir to the kingdom of Iolcus, a town in Thessaly, but the throne was usurped by Pelias, who was the brother of King Aeson, Jason's father. As a child, Jason had been entrusted to the centaur Chiron, who raised and educated him, as he had done with other famous heroes.

When he became an adult, Jason was recognized by King Pelias as the legitimate heir, and Jason claimed the throne that rightfully belonged to him. Pelias did not dare deny it but resorted to a ploy to get rid of him. Pelias promised to return the kingdom to Jason, on condition that Jason bring back the famous Golden Fleece, the golden ram's skin. This ram had been sent by the gods to save two children in the previous generation. It was guarded in Colchis.

The Fleece was dedicated to the god Ares and was hanging from an oak tree in a sacred grove, guarded by a huge dragon that never slept and that was wrapped around this tree.

Pelias thought Jason would not come back alive from this deed, but the young man did not lose heart. He built the ship Argo and took with him the bravest men of the time, (fifty-two and many others who joined during the trip), who were called Argonauts.

He went with them to Ea, the town where the precious fleece was kept. The journey was long and full of pitfalls. Jason and his companions had to bear trials and difficulties of all kinds, performing memorable feats, but eventually they reached their goal.

They were welcomed by King Beta, but when he learned that the purpose of the visit was the conquest of the Golden Fleece, he imposed a tough test on Jason: he would have to yoke two bulls that snorted flames from their nostrils, use them to plow some land, then sow the dragon's teeth and finally kill the warriors who would be born from those teeth.

The hero succeeded with the help of Medea, the king's daughter, who gave him a magic ointment because she was a witch. So Jason seized the fleece and fled with her. They returned to Iolcus, but Pelias did not give the kingdom back to him, breaking his word. Then Medea killed Pelias and with Jason had to leave the city. They fled to Corinth and lived there for many years until Jason tried to leave Medea to marry Creusa (or Glauce), the daughter of King Creon.

The sorceress Medea then exacted a terrible revenge: she killed Creon, Creusa and the sons she had with Jason, in order to punish Jason. The hero, deeply saddened, was condemned to wander the world until he was old. He died at Corinth, struck accidentally by a beam of the Argo, which had remained aground on the beach.

Analysis and unserstanding

1) To whom had Jason been given as a child?
2) What did King Pelias do when Jason grew up?
3) What was the most difficult feat demanded by Pelias?

4) Where was the Golden Fleece guarded and who guarded it?

5) What was the name of the ship that Jason built? And what was the name of his group of companions?

6) What trial did King Beta impose on Jason?

7) Who helped Jason in the enterprise?

8) What did Pelias do when the hero returned to Iolcus?

9) What terrible revenge did Medea carry out?

10) According to legend, what became of Jason?

Reworking and Writing

1) Even a myth that we mentioned earlier tells of dragon's teeth that needed to be planted and from which are born warriors. Find what this myth is, and explain orally in which of the two legends this episode is secondary.

2) Over the years the figure of Medea has inspired many artists. Do a search on the subject, including the names of artists and works that mention Medea.

Heracles and the Twelve Labors

Heracles was the son of the god Zeus and a mortal, Alcmene, wife of the king of Thebes. She had twins: Heracles, who was of divine lineage and Iphicles, who was mortal. This provoked the jealousy of the wife of Zeus, Hera, who even before Heracles was born prepared herself for revenge. Having learned from Zeus that one who would rule over the cities of Tiryns and Mycenae was about to be born, Hera turned to her daughter Eileithyia, the goddess of childbirth. Hera made sure that the birth of Heracles was delayed and the birth of Eurystheus, a cousin of Heracles, was early, so that Eurystheus became king, being born first, and not Heracles.

The legend says that Alcmene, fearing the terrible wrath of the goddess Hera, did not have the courage to keep him with her and left him in a field. Hera passed right over that place, and not knowing who the baby was and finding him very nice, decided to take him and nurse him. But the infant, perhaps already sensing the hatred of the goddess, gave a bite so that she screamed and pushed him away, so a spray of milk spread across the sky, forming the Milky Way. Not content with this, conscious of whom really the child was, the goddess even made an attempt on his life, trying to kill him when he was still in the cradle. She sent two huge snakes for this purpose. They bound him with their coils, but the child, with the strength of his own hands, was able to strangle them, thereby demonstrating superhuman strength and, therefore, to have a divine origin.

When Heracles was grown, he had many teachers, who taught him literature and music, things that were not suitable to him, and archery and the use of other weapons, things that could be much more fitting. From the centaur Chiron, he also learned medicine and surgery. Grown up, at just eighteen, he did the first of his heroic deeds, killing a lion on Mount Cithaeron that was decimating the cattle of the inhabitants, and that frightening everyone. Then he fought against the city of Orchomenus, which had imposed heavy taxes on Thebes. Thus, King Creon, to repay the valuable assistance provided by Heracles in the war, gave him his daughter Megara.

By Megara, the hero had many children, but Hera, who had not desisted from revenge, sent him Madness. The hero went out of his mind and killed all the children, whom he had mistaken for enemies. When he came to his senses, he was horrified by what he had done, and exiled himself from the world. He then followed the advice to go to ask the oracle of Delphi how to atone for the horrible crime. The oracle ordered him to be at the service of his cousin Eurystheus, king of Argos.

Eurystheus asked him to perform the twelve labors, and other deeds, and was encouraged to do so by the goddess Hera. Heracles was able to do them, always coming back to his homeland safe and sound. The oracle had also predicted that as compensation for performing twelve labors, he would be granted immortality. And indeed, it was so.

1. The first of the twelve labors that Heracles had to perform was the killing of the great Nemean lion. This lion lived on the plain of Nemea and was the son of Echidna, a monster with a woman's body on top and the tail of a serpent on the bottom. The lion was the brother of the Sphinx of Thebes (who had a human face, a lion's body, and wings) and many other monsters.

Heracles strangled the beast with his own hands, having noted that it was impossible to win with traditional weapons, such as the bow, the sword and cudgel. At the suggestion of the goddess Athena, Heracles then tore the skin with animal's own teeth, allowing him to skin it. With it, he made an indestructible armor, while with the head, with its open mouth, he modeled an invincible helmet. In fact, the hero is always depicted covered by the skin of the Nemean lion, along with the cudgel that he had made.

2. The second labor was the killing of the Hydra of Lerna, a many-headed monster (some say five, others one hundred, but most say nine), with the body of a snake. It was the son of the monster Echidna, too, as was the Nemean lion. It lived in a swamp, terrorizing local residents, looting crops and killing men with its mephitic breath.

Heracles saw that every time he cut off a head of the monster, it grew back, so he asked his faithful equerry Iolaus for help. He set fire to a nearby forest and obtained embers with which he burned every wound as Heracles cut off the heads, preventing them from regrowing.

Then the hero killed a giant crab sent by Hera and was able to return home safely and as the winner of the battle. Before leaving, however, the hero dipped his arrows in the poisoned blood of the monster, making them deadly weapons that were able to cause wounds that could never heal.

3. Then Heracles, on the orders of Eurytheus, captured alive a large wild boar that lived in the mountains of Erymanthian in Arcadia and led it to Mycenae.
After it tired, he placed it upon his shoulders and took it alive to the palace of Mycenae.
At the sight of the beast, King Eurytheus, scared, hid in one of the large jars placed on the ground near the throne room and begged Heracles to take the wild animal away.
During this labor, Heracles stopped to see his friend, the centaur Folo who lived in a cave, and although he ate nothing but raw meat, he was good.
The centaur received him amicably and offered him a rich banquet.
Heracles asked for some wine, but the jar that Folo had, belonged to all of the centaurs.

Unable to resist the insistence of Heracles, Folo opened the jar and offered wine to him, but the exciting aroma of the wine spread all around the cave and drew other centaurs from all sides.

Infuriated, they plunged into the cave, destroying everything and waging a fight with Heracles.

In the battle, Folo lost his life when he was wounded by one of Heracles's arrows that, as we know, he had dipped into the poisonous blood of the Hydra.

4.   The Ceryneian hind was bigger than a bull and had golden horns and hooves.

Four other hinds, just like her, had been captured by the goddess Artemis, who had yoked them to her chariot, leaving fifth one free to roam Mount Cerynea.

Heracles chased her for about a year, even though the animal had a phenomenal speed, reaching the extreme north and the land of the Hyperboreans.

He captured her only when the deer stopped, exhausted. After, he wounded her slightly with one of his arrows.

Then he loaded her onto his shoulders and went to the palace of Eurystheus.   Artemis and Apollo stopped him to claim ownership of the animal and accused him of trying to kill a sacred animal, an act that was considered very unholy. Heracles told them it was the order of Eurystheus and made it clear that he was not acting of his own volition to kill a deer, but he had wounded her only accidentally.

He was then allowed to leave with the captured deer because the two gods were convinced of his innocence.

5. In a dense forest near swamp Stinfula, a large flock of birds lived. Their feathers were colorful but sharp and pungent, so much so as to kill those who had approached them. Their claws, beaks, and feathers were made of bronze. They ravaged the lands around and pierced men.

With the help from the goddess Athena, who had the god Hephaestus make a bronze rattle, Hercules frightened the birds that rose in flight in a disorderly manner, so that the hero could easily destroy them.

6. With the sixth labor, Heracles had to clean up the stables of Augeas, king of Elis, where he had accumulated manure of numerous herds. Augeas had innumerable herds kept in his stables, and had forbidden anyone from approaching, out of fear that they would steal them. So no one had tried to clean the stables.

The hero bet the king he'd do it in a single day, and Augeas, convinced that the hero could never accomplish the feat in such a short time, promised him a tenth of his oxen.

Heracles then broke through the boundary wall and directed the flow of two rivers, the Alpheus and the Peneus, so that the stables were cleaned by the rivers in one day as he promised.

The legend goes on to say that Augeas knew he had lost the bet, but he would not respect the agreement. Indignant Heracles then killed him.

7. On the island of Crete, a raging bull devastated fields and crops. Poseidon had sent the animal to King Minos, but then caused it to be infuriated when the king failed to keep his promise to sacrifice to Poseidon.

Then it spread terror on the island. Heracles, obeying Eurystheus, sailed to the island and immobilized the animal using only a snare. Then he took it to Eurystheus, who wished to consecrate it to Hera, but the goddess refused to accept it, because of her grudge against the hero.

Eurystheus then let the bull go free, but the animal caused death and damage until he was killed by the hero Theseus at Marathon.

8. Heracles then had to tame four wild mares that belonged to the king of Thrace, Diomedes. They

fed on human flesh, and every foreigner that dared cross the kingdom's borders was fed to them.

To tame them, the hero fed them their master, Diomedes, and so was able to easily bring them to the palace of Eurystheus; the king left them to graze around Mycenae.

9. In the remote and mysterious regions of the North, in the Caucasus, lived the warlike people of the Amazons, who were warrior women.

Their queen was Hippolyta, daughter of the god Ares, who had given her a magnificent belt as a symbol of power.
The daughter of Eurystheus, Admeta, wanted this precious object at all costs, so Eurystheus assigned Heracles the task of procuring it. The hero set out with some friends including Theseus and Peleus.
Upon arriving he was greeted amicably by the Amazons and their queen, who would had even given up the belt without opposition if the goddess Hera had not infiltrated among the women, suggesting to Hippolyta that Heracles wanted to kidnap her.
A bitter battle then broke out, in which Heracles was able to kill the queen and seize her belt.
He then took it to Admeta, who dedicated it to Hera, whose priestess she was.

10. The tenth labor consisted in capturing and bringing to Eurystheus the herds of cattle owned by the monster Geryon, who looked like a winged warrior with three bodies and who lived in the far West. The animals were guarded by a giant shepherd and a two-headed dog.

By borrowing the sun's vessel with which the god Helios reached his home every night in the eastern world, Heracles managed to reach his destination.

During the journey, he came to the Strait of Gibraltar, which separates the Mediterranean Sea from the Atlantic Oceanus, and he erected there the two columns that bear his name (that have been associated with the two mountains that arise on both sides of the strait).

Having arrived in the country of Geryon, he managed to get the better of all the guardians of the herds, and of Geryon. Heracles was able to bring back the beautiful oxen with tawny fur.

During the return trip, he had to overcome other difficult tests, such as an attack by robbers who wanted to steal the oxen, and a horsefly sent by the goddess Hera, which did disperse part of the cattle.

11. The eleventh labor was to capture Cerberus, which was also the son of Echidna, as were the Nemean Lion and the Hydra of Lerna. Cerberus was a three-headed dog with a serpent's tail that

lived in the Underworld. Cerberus prevented the living from entering and prevented the dead from leaving.

A prophecy said that Cerberus could only be defeated with the help of the gods.

Heracles then enlisted the help of Hermes and Athena and purified himself with magic rites.

He then went into Hades, defeated the monster with the strength of his bare hands and arms, and carried it to Eurystheus; but, terrified at the sight, he asked the hero to take it right back.

And so it was, Cerberus took its place in the underworld and continued to be the guardian of the dead.

12. The last labor was to seize the apples of the Hesperides, the Nymphs of the Evening, who were in a wonderful garden at the western edge of the world, guarded by a dragon with a hundred heads, Ladon. Heracles did not know what direction to take to get there, so he forced Nereus, a god of the sea, to reveal it.

He was also advised to not take the apples himself, but to get help from Atlas, the Titan who had been forced to carry the world on his shoulders. Going to Atlas, Hercules offered to replace him for a while, if the Titan would gather the apples in the meantime. Atlas did not truly seem to be able to lift that burden from his shoulders, so he accepted.

Quickly he defeated the dragon and returned to Heracles with the precious apples.

When the hero was about to return the sky to him, Atlas refused to take back the charge, and said that he would bring the apples to Eurystheus. Heracles knew that he had fallen into a trap, and in turn acted cunningly: he pretended to accept and asked to weave just a pillow on which to rest the sky, for a softer support. Atlas naively took back the world on his shoulders, then Heracles promptly grabbed the apples and left, to take them to Eurystheus.

The king gave them to the goddess Athena, who in turn handed them back to the Nymphs because the divine apples could not stay outside of the gardens of the gods.

Analysis and Understanding

1) Whose son was Heracles?
2) Why did his mother abandon him?
3) What was born from the milk of the goddess Hera?
4) How then did she try to kill him?
5) Who taught Heracles medicine and surgery?
6) Why at some point did he slay all his children by Megara?
7) What did the oracle advise him to do to atone for his guilt?

8) What was he promised in return for completing the twelve labors?

9) Who was he to kill in the second labor?

10) What was he to bring to Eurystheus with the tenth labor?

Reworking and writing

1) Give a short title to each of the twelve labors, then summarize them in a short text.

2) The Hydra of Lerna is another terrible monster, after the Gorgon Medusa killed by Perseus and the Chimera killed by Bellerophon. Select from each of these fantastic creatures.

3) Is Heracles only strong, or do his abilities include reasoning skills and cunning? Reply by making appropriate references to the text.

Other Deeds of Heracles

The hero takes part in a huge range of adventures and deeds; we already talked about his participation in the Gigantomachy, the struggle between the gods and the Giants, which was won by the gods thanks to his decisive contribution.

Then he participated in the expedition of the Argonauts, as previously told, recounting the story of Jason and the Golden Fleece; he fought also with the god Phoebus for possession of a sacred tripod (the tripod was a vase with three feet).

The following are the most famous of Heracles' other deeds.

Heracles and Caco

The following is not a Greek legend, but Latin. It is linked anyway to the Greek hero Heracles, who was known and loved all over the ancient world.

In the Aeneid, the Roman poet Virgil tells the story of a confrontation between Caco and the hero. Caco lived in a cave on the Aventine, he was the son of the god Hephaestus and was a shepherd with a monstrous appearance.

Caco had stolen some cattle from the herd of Geryon, while the hero was taking them across Lazio to Eurystheus. In order not to have the place where he had hidden them discovered, the thief pulled the beasts by their tails, making them walk backwards until they were locked in his den. Heracles, very angry at the theft, immediately began to look for the animals, and suddenly he heard the roar of one of his oxen, which had responded to his call.

The roar came from the cave, but it was closed by Caco with a huge boulder. The hero did not lose heart and tore off the top of a mountain and pried open the entrance to the cave. Caco tried to defend himself spewing fire and smoke from his mouth, which caused a thick, dark fog. But Heracles did not appear intimidated; he jumped through the fire, grabbed the monster and squeezed him so hard that his eyes burst from their sockets.

The local people, grateful that the hero had delivered them from the monster, devoted a splendid altar, the Ara Maxima, to him, thus giving life to the cult of the hero in Italy.

Some saw in this myth a reference to volcanic phenomena present on the ground in ancient Lazio.

Heracles at the Crossroads

Legend has it that one day, when Heracles was still young, he was walking thoughtfully near Mount Cithaeron and was wondering about his future when two women - Pleasure and Virtue- showed up.

They represented the different paths that fate would have had in store for him, requiring him to choose one or the other.

The first woman invited him to follow her, because she would give him material comforts and wealth. The second one offered him a lifetime of work and struggle, even with some worries, but in the end he would achieve glory.

The hero did not hesitate: since he was wise, he chose the arduous path of virtue over pleasure, thus achieving fame and immortality.

Often in tales, even in the most modern fables, you arrive at a crossroads, which symbolize a choice between two different paths or solutions.

This legend wants to emphasize the importance of making the right choice.

Heracles and Hesione

Legend has it that King Laomedon of Troy, to build the walls of his city, had received the help of two gods, Phoebus and Poseidon.

Before starting the work the two had agreed upon a fee with the king. However, when it was over, he would not keep his promise, saying that nothing had been promised and nothing was owed. Then Phoebus, enraged, went up on the hill that overlooked the town and struck it with many arrows that caused a terrible plague.

Poseidon instead, slamming his trident on the sea, let out a terrible monster that started ruining crops and slaughtering men. Questioning the oracle of Delphi, the Trojans knew that the blame for everything that was happening was to be found in the oath not kept by their king, Laomedon.

To placate the wrath of the gods they had to sacrifice the beautiful daughter of the king, Hesione. Then the poor woman was chained to a rock on the shore, waiting to be devoured by a sea dragon.

Fortunately, Heracles was going that way just then, and seeing the girl, inquired what was happening. At once, the hero offered to free the city from the monster if the king would give him the girl in marriage.

As usual Laomedon promised, but the king would not listen to him when Heracles went to him to get his reward after killing the dragon. Then the hero, outraged, promised that he would return to take revenge, having something else to do at that time.

And so he came back with other Greek heroes after a few years, bringing war to the town of Troy, sacking the city and killing King Laomedon and his children, except Hesione, whom he gave as a bride to Telamon, his friend. Heracles spared her brother too, Podarces, the youngest son of Laomedon, since Hesione had pleaded with him.

From that moment Podarces changed his name to Priam, "the redeemed", and became king of Troy.

Heracles and Alcestis

Admetus, king of Pherae in Thessaly, was known for his sense of justice and for the great hospitality with which he welcomed travelers.

When Phoebus was condemned by the gods to be the servant of a mortal for a year, on account of his having killed the Cyclopes, he became a shepherd in Pherae. He was treated very kindly by Admetus. So he helped Admetus to marry the beautiful Alcestis, daughter of Pelias, the king of Iolkos.

Pelias, as his daughter had many suitors, decided that he would give her in marriage to him who had done something extraordinary, that is yoking a boar and a lion to a wagon. With the help of the god Phoebus, Admetus succeeded and was able to marry Alcestis.

After some time, however, Admetus fell ill and it seemed there was no hope for him to stay alive. But Phoebus obtained an agreement from the Moire, the deities who presided over the life and death of men, that another mortal could go to Hades instead of Admetus.

No one wanted to sacrifice themselves, even the elderly parents refused to die in the place of the child; only his wife Alcestis, driven by her great love for her husband, offered to take his place. Then Thanatos, the personification of Death, accompanied the courageous woman to the underworld.

After a while, Admetus noticed that now life no longer had any meaning for him, without his dear wife. Again the providential help of Heracles came. Hosted by Admetus in his house, the hero, during a banquet, not knowing what had happened, drank and sang merrily, until he learned of the sad fate of Alcestis. He decided to help Admetus and to revive his wife.

He fell into the Underworld, he fought against the same death, and managed to gain victory, forcing him to agree to release Alcestis. Then he took the woman, veiled, to her husband, and Admetus, after some initial uncertainty, once the veil was taken off, recognized his beloved woman Alcestis.

The myth suggests how the greatness of love is able to overcome even death itself.

Heracles and Deianira

After completing the twelve labors, Heracles returned to his town, Thebes, and repudiated his first wife Megara (his sons by her had been killed by the hero, driven mad by his enemy, the goddess Hera, as we have said. Then he married Deianira, daughter of Oneo, king of the Aetolians, after competing with the river god Achelous to get her. By her Heracles had a son, named Illo.

One day, during a trip, having to cross a river, Deianira got help from the centaur Nessus and climbed on his back to reach the other side. But Heracles saw that the centaur was preparing to flee with his wife, and shot him with an arrow poisoned by the blood of the Hydra of Lerna, that he had killed during one of his memorable labors, and killed him.

Before he died, however, Nessus had convinced Deianira to dip a robe of her husband in his blood, saying that this was to obtain a powerful love potion. If necessary, it would make Heracles always faithful to her.

The woman followed the advice and later, when Heracles returned from an enterprise of war with the princess Iole, whom he had taken prisoner, fearing that her husband wanted to leave her, she thought of using the robe. So she sent it to her husband and as soon as he put it on, he was seized with excruciating pain so strong that he preferred death to that suffering.

He decided to end his life on a funeral pyre that he had prepared on Mount Eta, to which his friend Philoctetes set fire, out of pity for the dying hero, as he had asked. But Zeus, moved to pity by the demise of his beloved son, with a lightning killed his mortal part, while the immortal part was carried into the sky among the gods of Olympus. There Zeus gave Hebe, the cupbearer of the gods, to him in marriage and gave him the gift of eternal youth.

While on earth, the unfortunate Deianira, conscious of having been deceived by the centaur and having been the cause, albeit unwitting, of the death of her beloved, killed herself in turn.

Before dying, Heracles had given to Philoctetes, son of his great friend Peante, the magic bow with arrows dipped in the poisonous blood of the Hydra of Lerna, in gratitude for having set fire to the pyre on which he lay.

Philoctetes

Before Heracles died, he donated his bow and arrows to Philoctetes.

During the expedition of the Greeks against Troy, Philoctetes landed near the town of Crisa and went to pray in a temple. There he was bitten by a snake, receiving a bad wound which soon became infected and fetid. The snake had been sent by Hera, the eternal enemy of Heracles, to punish Philoctetes for having lent aid to Heracles on his deathbed.

Then, the companions of Philoctetes, unable to bear the terrible smell caused by injury, went to Odysseus (Ulysses) for advice. They decided to leave him on the island of Lemnos, with his bow and arrows, which would allow him to survive by hunting.

And so it happened, Philoctetes was left on the island for ten years, subsisting on the game that captured.

But the oracle Helenus, son of King Priam and brother of Cassandra, revealed that the Greeks would never have won against the Trojans if they had not had the help of Heracles' bow and arrows.

Then Odysseus and Neoptolemus went to the island of Lemnos and tried to seize the bow through guile, but in the end, Neoptolemus, driven by compassion, revealed all to the unfortunate Philoctetes.

Odysseus was angry, but Heracles appeared providentially, restoring calm and convincing Philoctetes to follow the two Greeks and help them storm the fortress of Troy.

Arriving in Troy, he was healed by Machaon, son of Asclepius: first the god Phoebus sedated him and then Macaone addressed the wound, curing it with a medicinal plant whose secret had been revealed to him by the centaur Chiron.

Philoctetes, completely recovered, used one of Hercules' arrows to kill Paris, the Trojan who had caused the war, having carried off Helen, wife of Menelaus, king of Sparta.

According to legend, after the conclusion of the war, the hero returned home, but then he went back to sea, going to the Calabrian coast, where he founded several Greek colonies, today's Strongoli and Cirò Marina.

Analysis and understanding

1) Where did Caco live? What did the Latins build out of gratitude?
2) Write a short text imagining the conversation between Heracles, Pleasure, and Virtue.
3) The episode of Heracles and Hesione recalls another similar tale, that you've already read. What myth is it?
4) What deed did Admetus have to complete?
5) Who volunteered to die in his place?
6) Another mythical character descended into Hades to take back a woman, but he was more unfortunate. Do you remember who he was?
7) Who wanted to kidnapp Deianira and was therefore slain by Heracles?
8) What did the centaur Nessus do before he died?
9) Where did the immortal part of Hercules stay?
10) To which hero did he give the magic bow and arrows?
11) What did a bad wound do to Philoctetes?
12) On which island was he abandoned? Why then did they go to take him back?
13) Who healed him?
14) According to legend, which colonies did Philoctetes found in Southern Italy?

Reworking and Writing

1) The Greek colonization was a vast movement of Greek citizens who, leaving their homeland, went to found new cities, on the coast of Anatolia (modern Turkey), in southern Italy and Sicily.
Find news on the subject; also use your history book to help.

2) There are numerous depictions of Heracles (or Hercules, as he was called by the Romans). Do a search on the subject.

Sisyphus, who tricked Death

Sisyphus was the son of Aeolus and was the founder and first king of the town of Corinth.
He was very smart; many thought he was the cleverest of mortals. It is said, for example, that one day his cattle were stolen, and to make them unrecognizable, the thief painted them with different colors, but cunning Sisyphus was able to expose him just the same because he had previously put his brand under the animals' hooves. But his problems began for him later, when he incurred the wrath of the gods, especially that of Zeus, the king of the gods.
Zeus had kidnapped the beautiful nymph Aegina, who was the daughter of the river god Asopus and granddaughter of Oceanus and Tethys.

Sisyphus had witnessed the abduction, and when Asopus, under the guise of an old man, asked for news of his daughter; he admitted seeing her but did not notice the identity of the kidnapper right away. Before doing so, Sisyphus had made him promise, in return for the information, a source of water for Corinth, his home town, where the commodity was scarce.

Asopus promised and Sisyphus told him then that Zeus was the kidnapper.

When the king of the gods heard the denunciation of Sisyphus, he asked his brother Hades, the king of the Underworld, to send Thanatos, Death, to take him and lock in Tartarus.

But the cunning Sisyphus, welcoming her with great cordiality, made her drunk and managed to put her in chains.

With Death chained no one died on the earth and no one descended into Hades.

Ares, the god of war, noticed, in fact, that during the battles no one died, and not tolerating this futility of battles and wars themselves, he intervened.

He freed Death from the chains and handed to her he who had chained her, with a mandate to take him to the Underworld.

The wily Sisyphus, however, had already prepared his plan: he knew that Hades, the god of the Underworld, wanted, funeral rites to be celebrated for all the deceased, on pain of exclusion from Tartarus.

So he ordered his wife not to bury him and not to show sorrow for his death, indeed to show joy for the fact of being a widow.

Not being buried he could not enter into Tartarus, but he stopped on the banks of the River Styx, the river of hell that is the entrance of the Underworld.

Here, pretending to complain about what had happened, he persuaded Hades, Persephone, and other infernal gods to send him back to earth, to provide for his burial and to punish his wife for being so impious.

The gods condescended and allowed him to return to the world of the living, but only for three days.

Of course, Sisyphus never came back to the Underworld, continuing his existence on earth until old age.

When he really died, as punishment, he was forced to push a huge boulder up the slope of a mountain, but, as soon as he reached the top, it fell down, forcing the poor man to push it again, in a continuous and arduous work, for eternity.

Even today we use the expression "Sisyphean task" to indicate a job that involves great effort and poor results.

Some people saw in this mythic representation, by the ancients, the eternal and constant ebb and flow of the tides.

Analysis and Understanding

1) How was Sisyphus able to understand that the stolen cattle were his?

2) What did he make Asopus promise in exchange for information about the abduction of his daughter?

3) Who sent Thanatos (Death), and why?

4) How did Sisyphus act in regard to Thanatos?

5) What god did Thanatos free from the chains?

6) What did Sisyphus order his wife to do?

7) What is the Styx?

8) What did he persuade Hades and the other deities of hell to do?

9) How long did the gods allow him to remain on the earth?

10) What punishment was imposed on him for disobeying the gods?

Reworking and Writing

1) Have you ever heard the saying "Sisyphean task"? Give some examples of work you could call Sisyphean.

2) Why do you think some people saw the myth of Sisyphus as representing the tides?

Midas, gold and donkey ears

Midas was a legendary king of Phrygia, son of Gordian.

When he was young, still in the cradle, a miracle occurred: a long line of ants was climbing over the crib and each ant in turn laid a grain of wheat between the lips of the infant. No one had been able to explain the phenomenon, except for a soothsayer who prophesied that after some time the child would become the richest man in the world. And so it happened.

One day, having become a great king, he helped Silenus, who was the companion and teacher of the god Dionysus and who had got drunk and had fallen from the back of his donkey into the palace garden.

Dionysus, in gratitude for the help given to his companion, granted King Midas one wish, which he would readily grant. Then Midas asked that everything he touched be turned into gold.

His request was granted, but Midas had not taken into account the consequences of this new power: in fact, everything he touched did turn into gold, including even the food that touched his mouth or the water he drank. So this situation could not be allowed to proceed.

Midas was then forced to ask the god Dionysus to end the effects of the benefit granted him, otherwise he would have died of hunger and thirst. The god granted his request and told him to go and bathe in the waters of the river Pactolus to purify himself. He did so, and once out of the water, he realized that his ability to turn things into gold had disappeared. According to tradition, from that day, the waters of the river became rich with gold.

Midas was also the protagonist of another adventure. One day the god Phoebus and the god Pan competed in a musical contest, both being convinced that they were talented musicians, to determine who of them sounded better. They decided to appoint as arbitrator, King Midas, and, after the concert, he gave the victory to the god Pan. Then enraged, Phoebus said that his ears had deceived him and, as punishment, he made him immediately grow a pair of donkey ears.

Poor Midas, ashamed, tried in vain to hide them with a hat, which he always wore, but he had to have his hair cut, when it grew too long, and he had to go to the barber. He had him promise, however, that he would not reveal anything of what he had seen.

The barber promised at the time, but one day, unable to remain silent and eager to share the secret with someone, he thought of digging a hole in the ground near a swamp, revealing the fact to the hole, that the king had donkey ears and afterwards, covering the hole.

So finally he broke free of the secret and thought he had done no damage, but in the spring, at the point where he had dug the hole, a thick clump of reeds grew, which swaying in the wind, whispered repeatedly, "Midas has donkey ears! Midas has donkey ears!"

So anyone who passed there heard the news, and this quickly spread among all the people; so Phoebus had completed his revenge.

Analisys and Understanding

1) What prodigious event occurred when Midas was still small?
2) What did the fortune-teller predict?
3) Who was the drunk that fell in his garden, and what was his name?
4) Who allowed him to make a wish?
5) What did Midas request and obtain?
6) Why did he then beg Dionysus to cancel the benefit granted to him?
7) Midas was the referee in the contest between which two gods?
8) Who punished him by making him grow two donkey ears?
9) What did the barber do to get rid of the secret?
10) How did the news spread that Midas had donkey ears?

Reworking and Writing

1) What lesson can we draw from the legend of King Midas who transformed everything into gold? Express your considerations on the matter.

2) Phrygia is a region of Anatolia (modern Turkey). Midas is a mythical figure, but there was also King Croesus, who really existed, and was known to be very rich. He was the king of Lydia, another region of Anatolia.

Even today, to say that someone is very rich, they say "as rich as a Croesus." It is said that Croesus was the first to use currency as a bargaining chip. Until then, trades were done through barter, namely the exchange of an asset with another asset.

Certainly money was not invented at a certain moment. There was a long process that led to its use. Do a search on the origins of currency and its spread among ancient peoples.

STRANGE AND WONDERFUL CREATURES

Sirens

The origin of the legend of the Sirens is very ancient. They were creatures who bewitched sailors by singing with sweet voices. They were represented as half female, half animal beings.
We now know them as half woman, half fish in the lower part of the body, but this depiction has not always been the same.

In the remotest antiquity, we find descriptions of Sirens as being half woman, half bird, who also sang. In these early appearances they were compared to Harpies, other mythological beings with half human and half bird bodies. It's likely that the myth first arose in countries far from the sea, and then, when the legend arrived in coastal countries, the magical creatures changed their appearance.

The Greeks believed in several legends about the Sirens' origin: some claimed that they were daughters of the river-god Achelous and the Muse

Melpomene; others that the Muse Terpsichore was their mother. Others said that before, they were normal women that had been so transformed by the goddess Demeter, to punish them for not stopping the abduction of her daughter Persephone by Hades.

Later the Latin poet Ovid said that they had been women and afterwards they became mermaids because they had asked the gods for wings, in order to search on the sea for one of their comrades who had been abducted by Hades.

Another widespread legend has it that they were born from the blood of Acheloos, the river god who had horns and a serpent's tail, when the hero Heracles cut off his horn during the fight that saw them opposed to him marrying Deianira. From the wound fell twelve drops of blood, or six according to others, that created the first sirens.

Most likely the Sirens are the personification of the dangers of the sea; the ancients imagined them always near reefs or rocks emerging from the sea.

Evidently the Oceanus's currents that often originated in these areas, and that caused boats to be destroyed on the rocks, had given rise to the myth of these creatures that attracted boaters and that fascinated them so much that they threw themselves into the water to follow them, thus finding death. With the cult of the Sirens, therefore, they sought to propitiate a safe journey through the many pitfalls that the sea had prepared.

The first author who sang about the Sirens in his poems was Homer, legendary poet, who according to tradition wrote the Iliad and the Odyssey.

In the Odyssey, which we know tells of the wanderings facing the Greek hero Odysseus (Ulysses) returning to Ithaca after the Trojan War, it is said that the sorceress Circe, who hosted Odysseus, recommended the hero beware of the song of the Sirens.

The hero wanted to leave the island of Circe, to resume the journey back home, and the sorceress put him against the danger represented by these strange beings, and she suggested plugging his ears, and those of his sailors with wax so as not to become victims of their seductive song.

Odysseus, who always desired to learn new things, decided to listen to the singing too, but firmly tied to the mast of the ship so that he couldn't break free and jump overboard.

However, he warned his comrades not to untie him for any reason, even if he urgently pleaded with them to untie him. This is what happened: Ulysses could hear the seductive song of the Sirens and not be haunted by it because he had been bound by his companions.

The ship, driven by sailors who did not hear the sweet song, since they had wax plugs in their ears, as expected, was able to move away without damage. Then the Sirens, after this failure, committed suicide by jumping off a cliff. We know the names of three of them.

Parthenope, whose body will be transported by the waves to the islet of Megaride (located opposite the town of Naples), gives her name to the town of Parthenope, on the overlooking headland, the first group of what will be the capital town of the Campania region.

The name of another siren, Leucosia, is given to the promontory of Punta Licosa, in Cilento, in Campania; the body of a third, Ligea, would land in Punta Campanella, on the Sorrento Peninsula.

The famous Li Galli islands, facing Positano and near the island of Capri, would be formed by the petrification of the bodies of some sirens.

Another legend which speaks of these wonderful beings is that of the Argonauts. We know that the expedition of the Argonauts, led by Jason, was out to win the Golden Fleece in far away Colchis. During the journey, they encountered the Sirens, who began singing to bewitch them.

The crew was rescued by Orpheus, the mythical singer, who was on the ship, and who started playing so melodiously that everyone listened to him, regardless of the Sirens. As in the Odyssey, offended, they threw themselves off a cliff and perished.

Analisys and Understanding

1) How were and are the Sirens still represented?
2) How were they represented at first, in the most ancient legends?
3) Who was Acheloo?
4) Why, according to legend, had Demeter punished them?
5) Who wounded Acheloo during a fight?
6) What in fact did the Sirens represent for sailors?
7) Which poet first sang of the Sirens in his verses?
8) What hero, besides Odysseus, was able to resist their seductive song?
9) How did the Argonauts save themselves?
10) What end did the Sirens come to in both legends?

Reworking and Writing

1) So Homer tells the story of Odysseus (Ulysses) and the Sirens in the twelfth song of the Odyssey; the sorceress Circe is speaking, advising the hero on how to avoid falling victim to these dangerous creatures:
"To the Sirens first you will go, they who bewitch all men who approach them.
He who is unaware arrives and hears the voice of the Sirens, never returns home to his bride and little

children joyfully surrounding him, but the Sirens bewitch him with a harmonious song, sitting on the lawn, swarming around the shore of rotting human skeletons; on the bones the meat comes apart. (…)

In the passage that follows, the Sirens speak and attract the hero with false promises: "Come here, soon, o glorious Odysseus, great glory of the Achaeans, stay the ship, hear our voice. No one ever walks away from here with his black ship, before they hear, honey sound, the voice from our lips; then full of joy he goes again and knowing more things ...

In the latter song, the same Odysseus says: "So they said, raising their beautiful voices, and then my heart wanted to hear, and I ordered my companions to untie me, nodding to them with my brows; but they fell to their oars and rowed on".

(Odyssey, Book XII)

Why did Circe say that the banks around the Sirens' rocks are full of skeletons?

With what false promises do Sirens try to convince Odysseus to stop the ship and to hear their song?

What is the behavior of the hero?

What would he do if he were not firmly tied to the mast?

2)   As for Parthenope, in another legend she is a beautiful girl, daughter of a Greek commander, Eumelus, who had departed from Greece with the

intention of founding a colony in Magna Grecia, that today is southern Italy.

During the journey, the ship was hit by a storm, and the girl died. In her honor then, it was decided to call the new town that they founded by her name.

Do a search on the Siren Parthenope and the origins of the town.

The Harpies

There are various versions of the legend of the Harpies, creatures with the face of a woman but with the body of a big bird (like a vulture), with sharp claws, matted hair and wicked eyes, sometimes depicted with a hooked beak. The word "harpy" comes from a Greek word that means "kidnap", as it was said that they kidnapped the shipwrecked in storms. In the beginning, in fact, they were considered as demons that were manifested in the form of stormy sea winds.

Some believe they were daughters of Taumante and Electra, others of Typhon and Echidna, and even on their number there wasn't agreement: in Homer they are of indeterminate number; in Hesiod they are only two; later tradition tells of three Harpies, whose names were: Aello, which means "Gale", Ocipete, "That flies fast", and Celaeno, "the Dark", a name that recalls the dark atmosphere of the sky during a thunderstorm (although Homer calls the third Podarge).

Subsequently, they were considered infernal gods who kidnap the souls of mortals to take into the kingdom of the Underworld.

Like the Sirens, Harpies also sang enchanting songs, which fascinated those who listened to them, so often these two creatures were equated. Listening to their song was very dangerous: the men were mesmerized and lost all desires; attracted to these strange beings, often they forgot everything and were prey of death. According to classic mythology, they lived on the Strofades islands, where they had been confined by Zeus.

The god used them at will to persecute his enemies when the need arose. In fact, the most famous legend that features the Harpies is one that speaks of Phineas, King of Thrace, who was punished by Zeus for his crimes. The head of the gods ordered the Harpies to steal from Phineas all the food that he prepared ahead, and to dirty with their droppings, all that they could not take away. Phineas was released by the Argonauts, namely two of them, Calaide and Zete, the sons of Boreas, who were called Boreads. In fact, the Argonauts wanted to know from the king which route they should follow for safe navigation. He promised to reveal it to them only if they would liberate him from that terrible scourge. A version of the myth says that Calaide and Zetes, who were also provided with wings, killed the Harpies, chasing them in the sky with their swords. Another version says that they were pursued to the Wanderers islands, which by that time were called Strofades, "islands of the turn". Another even says that while they were being killed by the Boreads, Iris intervened. Descending from the sky, she made them promise that they would leave Phineas in peace in exchange for their salvation. The Harpies agreed and they went to live far away, in a cave on the island of Crete. It is worth noting that even the two Boreads (sons of the wind Boreas) are considered gods of storms, whirlwinds, vortexes. So talking about the Harpies, one often speaks of winds, storms and shipwrecks because the imagination of the ancients personified these natural phenomena as adverse deities.

In the Odyssey, Harpies are considered winds that bring marine storms, which upset and kidnap. In the book I (vv. 239-242), Telemachus, talking about the father whom he believed dead, says:

"All the Achaeans would have made him a grave and his son would have won great glory in days to come. But the Harpies have swept him away and left without a trace: he is gone out of sight …"

The same lines are used in the book XIV by the swineherd Eumaeus, who speaks of his master Odysseus to a foreigner who asks for news, not knowing that the stranger is his boss who returned secretly to take revenge on the principes who took his place in the palace.

In another passage of the Odyssey (in cap. XX, vv. 77-78) Penelope, wife of Odysseus, addressing a prayer to the goddess Artemis, speaks of the Harpies as storms that had kidnapped the daughters of Pandareus to make them handmaidens of the Furies, the terrible Erinyes, goddesses, also winged, who personified revenge.

"Meanwhile, the spirits of the storm snatched away the maidens and gave them to the hateful Erinyes to deal with." In this case, it is not kidnapping the dying and dragging them in the afterlife. The abducted girls are alive, and they will remain alive in the realm of the underworld.

Then let us remember that there is also a somewhat different legend, in which the Harpies die by the hands of Heracles.

Analysis and Understanding

1) How were the Harpies depicted?
2) From which Greek word does their name derive and why?
3) At first were they considered gods of which natural phenomenon?
4) How many were they, and what were their names?

5) What did they do to bewitch men?
6) Where did they live according to the legend?
7) Who was punished by the Harpies for his crimes, by order of Zeus?
8) By whom was Phineus freed?
9) Calaide and Zetes, the two Boreads, children of wind Boreas, are considered gods of what?
10) What are the Harpies similar to in the Odyssey?

Reworking and Writing

1) In the work "Argonautica" by Apollonius Rhodius (vv. II, 178-241, 262-300), the poem that speaks of the expedition of the Argonauts and the ship Argo, they tell of the Harpies. Read what the poet says about: " Phineas, son of Agenor, lived on the shore. Among all men he suffered the most atrocious punishments because of the gift of prophecy that the son of Leto once gave him. He did not have any restraint even to reveal to men the sacred thoughts of the son of Cronus. Therefore the god gave him a long old age, and he took away the sweet light of the eyes and did not permit him to enjoy the many foods that the neighbors brought him, asking for a prophecy; because, bearing down through the clouds, the Harpies always tore them from his hands and mouth with their beaks and sometimes they left him nothing, or sometimes only a little food, but he went on living and suffering. But there they spread a disgusting smell,

and no one could even bring food to his mouth or even stand the smell from a distance, such was the stench given off by the remains of the meal. But when he heard the voice, the roar of a group of men, he knew that those who had come would give him, according to the prophecies of Zeus, the joy of food."

The Argonauts come to his kingdom, and they ask directions on the route to be followed; Phineas promises to help them if they free him from the Harpies.

Then to attract the monstrous creatures, the Argonauts prepare a banquet and put it on hold:

"The old man had barely touched his food when, like growing storms or like flashes coming from the clouds, they pounced on it and eagerly shredded it with loud shrieking: at the sight the heroes gave a cry, but those, always screeching. They devoured everything, and flew away over the sea there was nothing left but an unbearable smell.

Then the two sons of Boreas brandished swords and pursued them.

Zeus gave them a tireless force: without him, they could never follow them because theyalways flew fast as storms of Zephyr when they went to Phineas or off again. Like when on the mountains, expert hunting dogs run on the slopes of the goats or deer, they push on with teeth clenched in vain, so the sons of Boreas closing in on the Harpies they tried in vain, stretching their fingers, to take them.

When they later reached them, far away in the Wanderers Islands, certainly they would have them smashed to pieces against the divine will, if the fast Iris had not seen them and not come down from heaven. She had stopped admonishing them saying: "It is not lawful, sons of Boreas, to hit the Harpies with your swords. They are the dogs of the powerful Zeus, but I swear they will not come back to Phineas." She said that and swore on the water of the river Styx, that for all gods is the most venerated and terrible, that never again would they go to the house of the son of Agenor; this was fated.

And they surrendered to the oath and quickly looked back to return to the ship; hence people gave the name of Strofades, Islands of Turn, to those that were first called Wandering".

After reading the text, write a short summary.

The Centaurs

The Centaurs were unique creatures, with a human torso and the body of a horse, who lived in the mountains and in the forests, feeding on raw meat and keeping rude and violent customs.

They were the offspring of Ixion and Nephele, but two of them, Chiron and Pholus, were different from their companions. They had a mild and wise character and did not resort to violence. On the contrary, they were experts, especially Chiron, in a number of arts and knowledge, including medicine. In fact, Chiron was the master of Heracles and many other heroes, like Theseus, Diomede, Jason, Achilles, Odysseus, Aeneas, etc. Even the gods Asclepius and Phoebus would receive, according to some, his lectures.

The founder of the Centaurs (except for Chiron, who was the son of Cronus, and Pholus, who was the son of Silenus) was, as we said, Ixion. He was guilty of a terrible crime. He was the first murderer of a relative because Ixion had made his father-in-law, Dioneus, the father of his wife Dia, fall into a pit of fire. Ixion had made a promise to his father-in-law, that is, to give him gifts in exchange for his daughter's hand, but then he had not kept his promise. Dioneus then asked him to keep his word and oath made in the name of the gods. But Ixion, who had no intention of keeping his promise, in order not have anyone know that he had perjured himself, killed him. No one could purify Ixion from this horrendous crime, and he eventually repented and went mad because of his remorse.

After a bit of time, however, Zeus, driven by compassion, released him from madness and, magnanimously, even hotsed him at the table of the gods. Here, however, Ixion tried to approach the wife of Zeus, Hera, who complained of this to her husband. The king of the gods then fashioned a cloud, Nephele, in the likeness of Hera, and Ixion, deceived by her appearance, had a son by her, Centaur, who in turn gave rise to the Centaurs. Ixion was then punished by Zeus; legend has it that he was tied to a wheel of fire that ran continuously in the sky.

The brutality of the Centaurs and the struggle they waged with the Lapiths is famous. The Lapiths were a people of Thessaly, and Pirithous was their king. It was said that the Lapiths were related with the Centaurs because their ancestors Lapite and Centaurus were twin brothers. Lapite was a skilled warrior, and his descendants were credited with the invention of bridles for horses.

On the occasion of his marriage to Hippodamia, Pirithous invited all the gods (except Ares and Eris, the gods of war and discord), and all the Centaurs; but since there was not room for everyone in the palace, the Centaurs were placed in a vast cave with some Thessalian princes. But the Centaurs were not used to drinking wine (they didn't even dilute it with water, as was customary at the time), so they got very drunk.

When the bride showed up to greet the guests, one of them, Eurytion, completely drunk, jumped from his seat, grabbed her by the hair and tried to drag her away.

Pirithous, aided by Theseus and other heroes, quickly came to the aid of Hippodamia, beginning a vigorous fight against all the Centaurs, who were eventually defeated and were forced to abandon Thessaly.

This episode was said to be the origin of the ancient enmity between the two peoples, the Lapiths and the Centaurs, inflamed by the gods Ares and Eris, as revenge for not having been invited to the wedding feast of Pirithous.

Analysis and Understanding

1) The Centaurs are often depicted as violent beings. Only two of them are not; in fact, they have knowledge in various arts and even in medicine. What were their names?
2) Whose teacher was Chiron?
3) From whom did most of the Centaurs descend?
4) What crime did Ixion commit so that he asked for forgiveness from the gods? Was he forgiven by them?
5) What was Ixion's punishment?
6) Against which people did the Centaurs fight?
7) What was the occasion that sparked the fight of the Centaurs?
8) Why did the Centaurs get drunk?
9) How did the fight of the Centaurs finish?

10) The gods are often portrayed as vengeful; also in this case, the fight is due to the revenge of two gods. Who were they?

Reworking and Writing

1) The murder by Ixion is not only against Dioneo, but also against the rules imposed by society. Not keeping an oath, especially in those days, when there was no written form, was a very serious act. Therefore Ixion is guilty also of diminishing the rules of civil society, i.e. the rules imposed by social relations, for living in the community. Explains this concept in your own words.

2) Try to trace the family tree (the list of ancestors) of the Centaurs.

3) Make a table with the names of the heroes who were students of Chiron, with their most important deeds.

The Cyclopes

According to Greek mythology, the Cyclopes are gigantic beings, with superhuman strength, who have the distinction of having one eye on the forehead.

The name means "round-eyed." In archaic Greek legends we can distinguish three generations of Cyclopes: the first giants are sons of the gods Uranus and Gaea (Heaven and Earth) and are present in the myths that speak of the formation of the world and the struggle for power, which will end when supreme command will pass to the god Zeus.

Tradition holds that Gaea begot three Cyclopes, one-eyed giants, builders of walls and expert locksmiths: Bronte (Thunder), Steropes (Lightning) and Arge (Flare).

Then there is a generation of Cyclopes builders, who were thought to have built the great megalithic or "cyclopean" constructions, as they are also called. According to legend, these Cyclopes lived in the caves of Sicily and the Aeolian Islands.

They had their forge under Etna, the volcano that is still active and periodically erupts from its mouth, smoke, lava and lapilli (a phenomenon considered then to have originated from the fire of the forge). Their blows on the anvils made the earth tremble, and their labored breathing formed the typical rumble which was heard outside from the throats of volcanoes.

They traditionally were the blacksmiths of the gods, under the direction of Hephaestus, the god of fire. They built the lightning for the chief of the gods, Zeus.

Zeus had struck the god Asclepius with lightning; he had been guilty of raising the dead with his medical arts, and for this reason the god Phoebus, the father of Asclepius, punished the Cyclopes by killing them and causing their souls to wander under Etna.

Zeus, angered, wanted to take revenge of Phoebus and send him down to Tartarus, the underworld, forever, but the mother of Phoebus, Leto, convinced him to forgive him.

There is another group of the Cyclopes who lived in Sicily, whom we find in the Odyssey. It is said in the Odyssey, the famous poem by Homer, that Odysseus (Ulysses) met them in Sicily, during his wanderings to return to his homeland, the island of Ithaca. In this famous episode, Ulysses was captured along with his companions by the Cyclops Polyphemus, but as usual, he cleverly gets out of the cave that the giant had closed with a giant boulder. In fact, the hero gets the Cyclops drunk by offering him excellent wine; then while he is dazed by alcohol, Odysseus blinds him with a sharpened stake. The problem of the rock that closes the mouth of the cave remains to be solved, but Odysseus devises a plan worthy of his cunning by hiding himself and his companions under the sheep that Polyphemus sends out the next morning for their usual daily grazing.

Despite the Cyclops checking by touch to be sure that only sheep and not men go out, he is deceived, for Ulysses and his comrades are well hidden under the sheep and careful not to be discovered.

Not even other Cyclopes could help Polyphemus, because when they asked who had blinded him, he replied "Nobody" as Odysseus had called himself at the beginning. So they turned away, although with some doubts about the strange things that were happening.

The Cyclopes described by Homer no longer work with iron, but they are wild creatures that live on sheep farming, raising sheep and rams, even practicing cannibalism, which for the Greeks was indicative of a primitive and crude state.

They live in caves, isolated from each other; they do not recognize any law nor worship any deity

Homer tells us the name of only Polyphemus.

Here is the description given in chapter IX:

"Here a man had cave, a monster, who fed flocks, alone, aloof, and did not mingle others, but lived alone, he had an unjust soul. He was a giant monster; and he did not look like a man who lives by eating bread, no, more like a forested peak..."

And again: "Poseidon who shakes the earth inflexibly is enraged over the Cyclops, the godlike Polyphemus, whom Odysseus blinded and whose

strength is greatest among all the Cyclopes."
(Odyssey, I, 68-71)

Someone thought that the legend of the Cyclopes was born from a primitive tribe or association of blacksmiths who had tattooed on their foreheads the image of the Sun, which gave the fire to their forges, symbolized by concentric circles; in recent times there is a growing hypothesis that the legend was born by the discovery of fossil remains of a variety of elephants that lived in Sicily during the Paleolithic Era. Their skulls in fact have a central hole, corresponding to the proboscis.

Ancient writers also speak of finds of giant bones, called "bones of Polyphemus," which would have belonged to a race of giant men.

They probably are the bones of large animals such as elephants or hippos, because scholars have found that in this ancient period these animals were present on Sicilian soil.

Analysis and Understanding

1) What were the names of the three Cyclopes to which Gaea gave birth?
2) What is the meaning of megalithic structures?
3) According to tradition, where did the Cyclopes have a forge?
4) What god directed them in their work as blacksmiths?

5) Which Homeric Hero met the Cyclops in Sicily?
6) What was the name of the Cyclops who imprisoned Odysseus and his companions in a cave?
7) How did the hero escape?
8) What did Odysseus tell Polyphemus his name was?
9) In what practice did the Cyclopes, including Polyphemus, engage?
10) What did cannibalism indicate to the Greeks?

Reworking and Writing

1) Research and briefly describe the episode of Odysseus and the Cyclops Polyphemus, as it's told in Homer's Odyssey.

2) Do a quick search on the animals that lived on Italian soil during prehistoric times, with particular reference to the Sicilian elephant.

The Moire

Among ancient Greeks, as among several ancient peoples, fate exerted great power over men. The Moire were the gods who presided over the fate of men, controlling their destinies.

They were three in number, and each one had her own role: Clotho (from the Greek word meaning "she who spins") kept the rock and pulled the thread and presided over births; Lachesis (which means "fate") wrapped the thread around the spindle, determining the fate and the duration of each person's life; Atropos, the last one, whose name means "the inevitable, the one from which there is no escape", had the task of cutting the thread, because she presided over death.

In the Orphic Hymns, it is said that they dwelt in a cave in the sky, near a lake formed by bright water flowing from a rock, illuminated by moonlight. In the Hymns it is also said that they are daughters of Ananke, Necessity, with whom not even the gods would dare dispute, and who is called "the mighty Moira".

Moira means "phase", and it is likely that there is a reference to the moon's phases. In ancient times there were three phases: the waxing moon, the goddess of spring; the full moon, the goddess of summer; and the waning moon, the divinity of autumn.

They don't often appear in Greek myths, but their existence is very important anyway. Some argue that, with the god Hermes, they created the alphabet, especially the first five vowels and consonants B and T. It was really they who then gave Hermes the ability to understand the alphabet.

Their work was final, everyone had to submit to their will, even the gods themselves, even Zeus. Only once it is said that Phoebus managed to make them drunk and make them change the fate of his friend Admetus, but this constituted an exception.

Some represent Atropos as the smallest of the three, but as the most terrible; Clotho holds a spindle or a book (obviously the book of fate), and Lachesis holds a stick pointing to a globe.

All three then are depicted as three very old women, looking serious, wearing crowns of woven flowers and wool, with white ribbons, and dressed in long white robes.

Their old age may be a symbol of the eternity of the divine will; the distaff and the spindle, the tools used for spinning, and the yarn are unquestionably the symbols of the course of life, which is unraveled; it grows slowly and then it ends.

In the tenth book of Plato's Republic, which speaks of the "myth of Er", a soldier who dies and goes to the hereafter and then comes back to tell the living what he saw, there is a representation of Moire together with the Sirens, depicting everyone in the act of singing: "The spindle revolved on the knees of Ananke. A Siren, emitting a single note of a single tone, moved up each of its wheels, but from all eight a single harmony rang. Three other women sat in a circle at equal distances, each on her throne. The Moire Lachesis, Clotho, and Atropos were the daughters of Ananke, dressed in white and her head crowned with bandages; on the harmony of the Sirens, Lachesis sang the past, Clotho the present, and Atropos sang the future."

The Romans called them Fates. Even in Scandinavian mythology there are similar deities known as the Norns.

Analysis and Understanding

1) Who were the Moire, and how many were there?
2) What were their names?
3) What was the name of the Moira who cut the thread?
4) Where was it said that they lived?
5) How is Ananke, Necessity, also called?
6) Which astronomical phenomenon is associated with them?
7) With which god did they compose the alphabet?
8) How was Clotho represented?
9) What did the Romans call them?
10) What were they called by the Scandinavian peoples?

Reworking and Writing

1) Among the Etruscans, the people who lived in Etruria, that is today's Tuscany, there was a deity that represented destiny. The Etruscans believed that heaven and earth were closely related and that the man had to submit to the will of the gods. However, he could interpret the will of the gods and predict the future through rites and ceremonies

performed by Augurs and Haruspices. Do a search on the subject.

2) In the myth of Er, it is said that a soldier, Er, is killed in battle, but that after twelve days he revives and tells his companions what he saw in the afterlife. The souls of the dead proceed in a row, to choose another life to lead on earth. The Moira Lachesis makes them choose in what form they want to be reincarnated; everyone chooses according to his will and his experience, but it is said that those who come after don't have to choose a worse life if they choose wisely. In fact, there many are existences under whose likeness one can come back to life. One can choose the life of a man, a woman, an animal, a tyrant, a simple person, a famous person or an unknown person. Then, after drinking water that makes one forget, all souls are sent back to Earth. Only Er does not drink, because he has the task of reporting to other mortals what he saw.
Do a search on the subject.

Typhon

Gaea, the earth, to avenge the killing of the Giants, gave birth to a new being, Typhon, the largest monster that ever existed, with stature and strength above all.

He had long arms, which had snakes' heads instead of hands, and when he extended them, one touched the East and the other the West. His lower body was all a tangle of snakes.

He had a donkey's head (some say even three) that touched the sky and wings obscuring the sunlight, and from his eyes came flames, and from his mouth spewed flaming rocks.

At some point Typhon, with all his enormous strength and eyes that sparkled with flames, began the assault on Olympus, contending with Zeus for world domination.

Then all the Gods, afraid of that terrible sight, fled to Egypt, where they took on the form of animals to avoid recognition: Zeus became a ram, Phoebus a crow, Dionysus a goat, Hera a white cow, Artemis a cat, Aphrodite a fish, Ares a boar, Hermes an ibis, etc.

Only Athena had the courage not to flee, even more, she almost scolded Zeus. Zeus then resumed his likeness, striking Typhon first with a flash of lightning, and then attacking him with a sickle.

Typhon, injured, engaged in a fierce fight with Zeus, wrapping him with his coils. Then he managed to get hold of Zeus's sickle and cut the tendons of his hands and feet, hiding them in a bearskin, guarded by his sister Delphine, a virago with a serpent's tail.

Then he dragged the god into a cave, where Hermes and Pan had managed to come and recover from the initial shock; while Pan frightened Delphine with a scream, Hermes seized the tendons of Zeus and put them back in their place.

Then Zeus returned to Olympus, and from his chariot pulled by winged horses, he began throwing countless thunderbolts against Typhon, who, to defend himself, hurled whole mountains against the god, but these were repelled by the thunderbolts of Zeus that struck Typhon, seriously injuring him and causing to run away, looking for a safe place.

When Typhon went to Mount Nysa, the Fates, the goddesses who presided over the destinies of men and gods, deceived him and offered him the fruits of death, which weakened him (apparently his fate was sealed).

To escape Zeus who continued to press him with his arrows, Typhon crossed the sea seeking shelter in Sicily.

Here his adventure ended because Zeus crushed the monster under Etna, which from that point began to spit fire.

The legend says that when Typhon tries to shake off the weight of Sicily, the ground shakes and earthquakes occur.

Other ancient authors point to Ischia as the island under which Typhon was imprisoned.

Note that Ischia is an island of volcanic origin too.

Still, others think that Typhon spreads himself under the whole region from Cuma in Campania to

Etna in Sicily, thus linking the volcanic phenomena of the whole area.

Here's how Hesiod describes him in Theogony: "Typhon was very strong: he had one hundred stalwart hands, disposed for every type of work, and one hundred tireless feet of god's strength; and he had a hundred heads of snakes and of horrible dragons, and one hundred livid tongues vibrated from all the horrible heads, under the eyebrows flaming with fire: when looked at, the eyes shined and the flames burned, when looked at, from all heads.

And when speaking, all the horrible heads emitted wonderful voices, of all species.

Now they spake so the gods understood them: the high bellows of a bull then came forth, bellows of immense force, of fair voice; then a lion of raw soul; afterwards there seemed to be the yelps of puppies, and to hear them you were amazed: then there were explosions, and the sublime Alps echoed".

Analysis and Understanding

1) Why did Gaea raise the gigantic monster Typhon?
2) Why did he begin the assault of Olympus?
3) Where did all the gods seek refuge?
4) Into what did they transform in order to hide?
5) What animal did Zeus turn (himself) into?

6) Who was the only god who did not flee, but rather scolded Zeus for having so little courage?

7) What was the name of Typhon's sister?

8) Who came to the cave where Zeus was held prisoner?

9) What did the god Pan do?

10) What weapons did Zeus and Typhon use in their last fight?

Reworking and writing

1) Do a paraphrase of the passage of Hesiod's Theogony.

2) Explain in your words why the ancients believed that Typhon had been crushed under Etna, or according to others, under the island of Ischia.

Echidna

She is one of the oldest monsters of Greek mythology, depicted as a being whose body was that of a woman from the waist up, and that of a snake on the rest, with a long tail.

Her name means "the Viper"; it is said that she to be was born from Ceto and Forco, according to some, or from Callirrhoe and Crisaore, according to others, and that she lived in a cave in Cilicia, in the country of Arimi, far from everyone.

She was the wife of Typhon, also called Typhoeus, another monster who was not bad, we could say jokingly, about whom we have talked before.

The two gave birth to a series of mythological creatures, all very bloody and terrible, like the Hydra of Lerna, the Chimera, the Sphinx, the dog Cerberus, Scylla, the dog Orthrus, the Nemean lion, the snake Ladon, who was guarding the apples of the Hesperides in the famous garden, the eagle that tortured the body of the giant Prometheus.

Indeed Echidna is often remembered just as the parent of these monsters, which caused many problems for several men and heroes, and the monsters were overcome after prodigious battles and various tricks.

Heracles in fact killed the Hydra of Lerna, the Nemean lion and the dog Orthrus and captured Cerberus, even if he did come back to Tartarus, where he remained to guard the kingdom of the underworld.

Bellerophon, with the help of the winged horse Pegasus, defeated the Chimera.

Oedipus, knowing how to solve the famous riddle of the Sphinx, forced the monster to commit suicide by jumping off a cliff.

Echidna then met the same death at the hands of Argus with the hundred eyes, the son of the god Zeus and the mortal Niobe.

In the Greek colonies of the Euxine, in today's Black Sea, another legend of Echidna also circulated, according to which the hero Heracles arrived in Scythia, went to sleep, letting his horses graze peacefully; but when the hero awoke he did not find the animals any more, which had been hidden by the monster.

Heracles went out in search of them and found them in the cave of Echidna, who, only after much persuasion, agreed to return them to their rightful owner.

To the ancient Greeks these mythological monsters of origins apparently accounted for obstacles that opposed the formation of a cosmic order; only through their defeat could a divine order be established on Earth.

In fact we see that all these terrible creatures are defeated by gods or heroes: Zeus is the same that eliminates Typhon through his thunderbolts; as we have seen, all others are defeated by various strong, brave and smart heroes.

A beautiful description of this strange and terrible monster is found in Hesiod's Theogony, vv. 295 et seq, when, speaking of the Titans, the poet mentions Callirhoe, daughter of Oceanus, who with Chrysaor parented Echidna:

"This woman gave birth to another invincible monster, in nothing similar to mortal men or immortal gods, in the hollow of a cave, the divine Echidna with violent heart, half-girl with shining eyes and lovely cheeks, but half prodigious cruel serpent, terrible and great, cunning, beneath the recesses of the divine ground; there she has the cave, down under the rock quarry, far from the immortal gods and the mortals, because there the gods gave her the illustrious house to inhabit, and it is in the country of Arimi, under the earth, the tearful Echidna, immortal young girl and evermore young, always.

Terrible unjust and violent Typhon was to her, they say, united in love, her bright-eyed girl, and she conceived and bore children of violent heart: Orthrus, Cerberus, Hydra, Chimera.

She still bore the nefarious Sphinx, ruin of the Cadmeans, lying with Orthrus, and the Nemean lion, who was fed by Hera, the noble wife of Zeus, who in the valleys Nemee did live, punishment for men, where dwelling destroyed the armies of men."

It is from Echidna and the ranks of monsters she generated, dragons from the Middle Ages originated; in fact, the dragon was often represented with the body of a snake, bat wings, and the head and paws of a lion.

In medieval Europe dragons have features of dangerous monstrosities. Conversely, in Eastern civilizations, such as in China or Japan, the dragon is a symbol of the sky. A beneficial being that brings rain and is considered a sign of life and renewal.

Analysis and Understanding

1) How was Echidna represented?
2) What does her name mean?
3) Where does it say that she lived?
4) What other monsters did she generate?
5) Who killed the Hydra of Lerna and the Nemean lion?
6) Who helped Bellerophon to defeat the Chimera?
7) What did the Sphinx end?
8) For the Greeks, these monsters were symbols of what?
9) Who eliminated Typhon and how?
10) What is the Euxine?

Reworking and Writing

1) Do a paraphrase of the passage of the Hesiod's Theogony which speaks of Echidna.

2) Find medieval images of dragons and try to draw one.

3) Do a quick search of the meaning of the dragon in the Eastern civilizations.

The Sphinx

The Sphinx is another mythological monster created by the imagination of the ancients.

She is a strange creature present both in Greek and Egyptian mythology, with a lion's body and a woman's head, but in the Greek myth she is almost always represented with wings.

Even her position varies between the two peoples: by the Egyptians she is depicted as a lion lying on the ground, while for the Greeks she is squatting on her haunches and has an upright torso.

In Egypt, statues of sphinx were located at the gates of the town, as if to watch over them.

It is written in the Book of the Dead, an ancient Egyptian sacred text, that she is "the keeper of the forbidden threshold and of the royal mummies. She listens to the song of the planets, waking on the edge of eternity, of all that was and will be. She sees the celestial Nile flowing in the distance and navigates the boat of the sun."

Even the colossal Spyhinx whom you can still admire in El-Giza, the Valley of the Temples, close to the three pyramids of Cheops, Chephren, and Mycerinus, probably had the task of safeguarding the entire valley.

The Sphinx of El-Giza, as several Egyptian sphinxes, has the head which depicts the face of the pharaoh.

The word "sphinx" means "strangler", and from her name we can understand what kind of creature she was.

According to Greek mythology The Sphinx is the monster offspring of Echidna and Typhon, or, according to others, of Echidna and Orthrus (Echidna, as we have seen, was another monstrous being, half girl, half snake, which generated a number of monsters, such as Chimera, the Gorgon, Scylla, Cerberus, etc.).

In Greece, the Sphinx takes on more cruel and enigmatic characters; legend has it that she was sent by the goddess Hera, wife of Zeus, against the town of Thebes, to punish King Laius, who was guilty of serious crimes.

She was placed on a rock, and from there she proposed riddles to those who passed, and those who could not guess were devoured.

The riddle that she proposed was: "What animal walks on four legs in the morning, two at noon and in the evening with three?" Today everyone knows the answer because the riddle and the solution became famous: it is a man. When he is a kid he walks with the help of his hands, and when he is old he walks with a cane. But back then no one could solve the riddle of the Sphinx and several were killed.

The Thebans promised the command of their city to anyone who could solve the riddle because it had been predicted that in this case, the Sphinx would die. The legend says that Oedipus gave the right solution, freeing the town of Thebes from this scourge. The Sphinx, in fact, defeated, committed suicide by jumping from the cliff and Oedipus became the lord of the town of Thebes.

Analisys and Understanding

1) What are the differences in the depiction of the Sphinx between the Egyptians and the Greeks?
2) Where is the famous statue of the Sphinx near the pyramids?
3) What is the face of the Sphinx in Egypt?
4) What does the term "sphinx" mean?
5) Whose the daughter was she, according to the legend?
6) Who sent her to Thebes and why?
7) Where did she settle and what was she doing?
8) Which riddle did she propose to passersby?
9) Who solved the riddle?
10) What did the sphinx do then?

Reworking and Writing

1) Do a search on the Egyptian Sphinx, which is located in El-Giza.

2) Find depictions of Egyptian sphinxes and Greek sphinxes and describe in your own words the differences you notice.

Cerberus

As we already know Cerberus was the son of Typhon and Echidna and the brother of the Hydra of Lerna, the Chimera, the Sphinx, the dog Orthrus, and other similar beings.

He's a dog that has three heads, which according to some symbolize the different ages of time, the past, the present and the future, with the throats always wide open, the tail of a serpent and sometimes snake heads on the back. In some versions of the legend he has more than three heads, some say fifty, others even a hundred.

He is at the entrance of Hades, the dark Underworld, on the bank of the river Styx, to which the souls of the dead go and from which they can not go back.

Cerberus has indeed been commissioned to check that no one enters the Underworld alive, and especially that no dead soul will come out. Only three heroes had the courage to deal with this monstrous creature. Heracles descended into Hades to bring back beloved Alcestis to her husband Admetus, and bound him to make him harmless. Orpheus descended into the Underworld to beg the god Hades to let his beloved Eurydice come back to Earth, and put him to sleep with the sound of his melodious lyre. The Latin hero Aeneas fell into the Underworld to meet the soothsayer Tiresias and ask about his fate. Cerberus dozed off with a magic cake of honey and herbs.

The souls of the dead as they entered the Underworld had to appease Cerberus with a cake made with honey. This cake was placed in the tomb for just this purpose.

Cerberus was also the protagonist of one of the twelve labors of Heracles. As we have seen, in obedience to Eurythstheus, king of Tiryns, the hero also had to complete the task of bringing him the hellhound Cerberus.

Heracles, after descending into Hades and beating him in the struggle with only the force of his arms, brought him to Eurystheus.

But he had to take him back because when the king of Tiryns saw the monstrous dog, he was filled with terror and hid, frightened. He ordered the hero to move away immediately with the beast. Cerberus was then taken back into Hades and returned to guard the kingdom of the Underworld.

In the Odyssey we find the story of this episode that the same Heracles, who had died and descended into Hades, does to Odysseus:

"And I was the son of Zeus, son of Cronus, but tears I had beyond measure: a man much lower I had to serve, and he ordered me painful labors.

One day he sent me down here, to take his dog: for he could devise for me no other task mightier than this! but I brought it, I pulled it out of Hades: and Hermes was my guide, and flashing-eyed Athena "...

(Odyssey, XI, vv. 621- 627)

Analysis and Understanding

1) Whose son was Cerberus?
2) How was he portrayed?
3) Where did he live?
4) What was his job?
5) Who among mortals dared to descend to Hades and challenge him?
6) How did Orpheus calm him?
7) What did the souls of the dead take to Cerberus?
8) Who defeated him in the fight?
9) What did Eurystheus do when he saw the monstrous dog?
10) What did Cerberus continue to do then?

Reworking and Writing

1) Paraphrase the above passage from the Odyssey.

2) With the help of the teacher, read the following passages about the dog Cerberus, taken from Virgil's Aeneid and the Divine Comedy by Dante

Alighieri; comment on them and note their differences.

Aeneas numbs the monstrous dog with a soporific cake that causes sleep, which the Sibyl, a sorceress who accompanies him in the Underworld, throws into the jaws of the beast:

"Once they came, they heard him the great Cerberus barking with three throats, and the realm of darkness stunned all; then in a huge cavern they saw first lying ahead, then he rose, gnashing, being rabid, with three necks he ruffled, and a thousand snakes shook around. Therefore the wise sorceress took the cake of honey and enchanted corn, such a soporific mixture, she cast it among the ravenous throats.

Greedy, ravenous and furious, opening the three mouths he guzzled the treat of honey and magic grain and sent it down the three throats and into the belly. With his six eyes closed by sleep that overtook his whole body, he lay abandoned and defeated in the cavern.
(Aeneid, VI, vv. 612-629).

Dante puts Cerberus guarding the circle of the greedy men and describes him thus:

"Cerberus, cruel and uncouth, with three throats like a dog barks over the people that are there submerged. He has ruby eyes, a greasy and black beard, and large belly, and armed with clawed hands; Scratching the spirits and flays and cuts

them ... When Cerberus perceived us, the great worm! opened mouths and showed teeth; Not a limb had he that was motionless."
(Divine Comedy, Inf. VI, vv. 13-24)

The Chimera

Even the Chimera, a mythological monster, is the daughter of Typhon and Echidna, and therefore sister of all other monsters which have already been mentioned.

The name in Greek means "goat". She is not always depicted in the same manner; she has features that can vary, but her body is always made up of parts of different animals. Some say she has a lion's head, a goat's head on her back and tail of a serpent. She spat fire from the mouth and her tail was poisonous. Others depict her with a goat's body, and sometimes with two heads. Others claim the Chimera has a lion's or goat's body and three flanked heads of a lion, goat and serpent, which develop from a single neck.

The legend says that she was raised by King Amissodore (or Amisodare) and for a long time, she terrorized the coasts of Caria, a region of Turkey, making continuous raids and wreaking destruction and pestilence. The hero Bellerophon succeeded with the help of the trusty winged horse

Pegasus, who took him on top of the monster so that they could not be reached by it.

Bellerophon dropped a piece of lead into the jaws of the Chimera, which melted in the fire that she was emanating, and ultimately choked her.

The Chimera was the personification of the storms, its voice represents the thunder and the unleashing of the elements.
In the Iliad we find a precise depiction of the monster:
"... She was the monster of divine origin,
Lïon's head, goat's chest, and dragon's
tail; and from mouth horrific blazes
vomiting of fire: and yet,
by favor of the gods, the hero turned it off ... "
(Iliad, VI, vv. 222-226)

Analysis and Understanding

1) Who were the siblings of the Chimera?
2) What does her name mean?
3) Was she always represented in the same manner?
4) What were her most frequent depictions?
5) Who raised her?
6) Which region did she devastate?
7) Who ordered Bellerophon to kill her?
8) Who helped Bellerophon?
9) How did the Chimera die?
10) Of what was she the symbolic representation?

Reworking and Writing

1) Paraphrase the Iliad's passage that tells of the Chimera.

2) With the help of the teacher explain what are the name and meaning of the two dots on the "i" of "lion" in the quoted passage of Iliad.

3) Explain in your own words why the Chimera was considered the personification of the storms.

Scylla and Charybdis

Scylla ("she who slays") and Charybdis ("she who sucks") are two sea monsters in Greek mythology who were at the opposite sides of the Strait of Messina, with the former on the Calabrian coast and the latter on the coast of Sicily. They are obviously the personification of sea swirls and the upheavals caused by storms in that part of the sea, which at that time had to be a serious problem for sailors. This myth, like many others that deal with the marine environment, concerns the sailor's fear in the face of hostile forces of nature, which he feels are threatening and powerfully destructive. Crossing a strait also meant leaving known places to venture into the unknown. Here, then, legends arose about monsters who were guarding the passage, who hindered the sailors from going further and who often devoured them.

Charybdis, who lived on a rock at today's Capo Peloro, Sicily, was the daughter of the sea god Poseidon and of Gaea (Earth), or, according to others, her parents were Forco and Gaea. She had been a woman who once was very voracious.

When one day Heracles crossed the strait with Geryon's herds, which he had caught during one of his labors. Charybdis devoured the oxen. Then the god Zeus punished her by hitting with one of his lightning bolts, by making her fall into the sea, and by turning her into a terrible sea monster. Since then, in fact, she swallowed large amounts of sea water three times a day. This water contained vessels that were passing through. She then vomited the ingested water.

Scylla instead, according to a legend, was once a beautiful young girl, daughter of Typhon and Echidna, who lived on the coast of Calabria, near Zancle, the present town of Reggio Calabria. She had the habit of going to the beach and swimming in the clear waters of the Tyrrhenian Sea.

One evening she saw a wave coming toward her, and in the waves appeared a strange figure, half man, half fish, with the blue body and green beard, with long hair full of algae. This creature had once been a fisherman named Glaucus. He had been turned into a sea god after eating a strange grass. The girl, frightened, ran to the top of a mountain not far away, but the god began to tell his story.

The sea gods had warmly embraced him, and Oceanus and Tethys had taken away even the last human forms, making him a divine creature. Scylla, however, was not moved by the adventurous story of Glaucus and ran even farther.

Then the god decided to go to the sorceress Circe, who lived on the island of Eea, to ask her to prepare a magic potion, to make the beautiful maiden fall in love with him. But the sorceress, who was secretly in love with Glauco, noting how great was his love for her rival, decided to take revenge and had it in a cruel way. When Glauco went away, she prepared a philter, but not of love, and went to pour it into the sea off the coast of Zancle. When Scylla was diving as usual, she noticed with horror that numerous heads of monstrous dogs emerged from the waters around her. She started to remove them, but she was even more horrified to see that those heads, six of them, with three rows of teeth for each face, had grown up on her legs and waved by moving their snake-like necks. Desperate, she decided to throw herself into the sea and to stay forever in a cave under a rock, in front of the cavity in which Charybdis lived.

Even Odysseus, who once passed through the Strait, had to make the acquaintance of two terrible monsters. He was sucked up by Charybdis, but he cleverly clung to a fig tree that grew at the entrance of the cave where the monster was hiding.

When Charybdis poured out the water she had swallowed, the tree also spilled out/rushed out and the Hero was able to save himself and resume his journey. But on the other side, Scylla was waiting for him, lurking in her dark room, and so six companions of Odysseus were first raised in the air and then devoured by the monster, but the hero could do nothing to save them.

This is how it is described in the Odyssey:

"Scylla lives there, horribly barking:

the voice is like that of a newborn bitch,

but she is scary monster,

nobody would be joyful to see her,

even a god, if they should meet.

The feet are twelve, all invisible:

and she has six long necks: and on each a head

to frighten; in the mouth three rows of teeth,

dense and tight, full of black death.

Half is hidden deep in the cave,

but she pushes the heads out of the horrible pit,

andthen they do her fishing and they rock around, poking around among the dolphins and sea dogs, and sometimes she grabs even larger monsters,

and a thousand of these feed the screaming Amphitrite.

The other rock, you will see it, Odysseus, is lower; you are close to each other; thou couldst even shoot an arrow across to it - and on it is a great fig tree with rich foliage, but beneath this, divine Charybdis sucks down the black water.

Thrice a day she belches it forth, and thrice she sucks it down terribly.

Mayest you not be there when she sucks it down, for no one could save you from ruin… […]

(Odyssey, Book XII, vv. 85 et seq. and 100 et seq.)

Scylla and Charybdis are also mentioned in the legend of the Argonauts, who managed to escape danger thanks to the intervention of the Nereid Thetis, mother of Greek hero Achilles.

Analysis and Understanding

1) What do the two names Scylla and Charybdis mean?
2) Where did the ancients imagine that they lived?
3) Why do you think this legend arose?
4) Why was Charybdis punished by Zeus?
5) How many times a day did Charybdis swallow

large masses of sea water?

6) What do you call today the ancient town of Zancle?

7) Who came from the sea one day while Scylla was on the beach?

8) Who was previously Glauco, then turned into a sea god?

9) To whom did Glauco go to prepare a love potion?

10) What instead did the sorceress Circe do and why?

Reworking and Writing

1) Scylla and Charybdis are personifications of two dangers that arise at the same time and which are unavoidable; even today "to be between Scylla and Charybdis" indicates that by avoiding one danger, you may fall into another.

Explain this saying in your own words, also using examples from your experience.

2) The Book XII of the Odyssey tells the story of Odysseus' companions devoured by the sea monster:

"...even so did Scylla land these panting creatures on her rock and eat them up at the mouth of her den, while they screamed and stretched out their hands to me in their mortal agony."

(Homer, Odyssey, Book XII, vv. 335-338)

In front of her, on the other side, was Charybdis:

"…and on the other dread, Charybdis kept sucking up the salt water. As she vomited it up, it was like the water in a cauldron when it is boiling over upon a great fire, and the spray reached the top of the rocks on either side."
(Homer, Odyssey, Book XII, vv. 309-313)

Paraphrase the above verses.

Argus

Argus, who was nicknamed "Panoptes" meaning "one who sees everything," was a giant with prodigious strength. According to some, he was the son of Mother Earth, and had the distinction of having more than two eyes. Some versions of the legend speak of four eyes, two in front and two in back, other than an infinitey number of eyes spread throughout the body others mention a hundred eyes, not well located. This allowed him to be attentive to what was going on around him, because when he fell asleep he closed only half his eyes, while the others remained vigilant.

He is remembered for freeing the region of Arcadia from a giant bull and from a Satyr that was ravishing herds, and also for killing the monstrous Echidna, the half woman, half snake creature.

The legend in which he is the protagonist is the one that tells the story of the beautiful Io, a comely maiden daughter of Inachus, king of Argos, and of the nymph Melia. She was so beautiful that the goddess Hera was jealous, and to avoid problems with his wife, Zeus, her husband, decided to turn the girl into a white heifer.

Hera, who was not trusting, asked her husband for custody of her, and Zeus, in order to not make her suspicious, acquiesced to her request. The goddess Hera then named as guardian of the beautiful Io, who had been turned into heifer, the giant Argus with a hundred eyes. This tied the poor animal to an olive tree growing in a sacred forest near the town of Mycenae, and thanks to his countless eyes he could not lose sight of her, because when he rested only some of them were closed.

The god Zeus could not bear that Io had been subjected to such a pitiful state. He then called the god Hermes, the messenger of the gods, and commissioned him to free the girl. Hermes, disguised as a shepherd, arrived like lightning on the meadow where the heifer was grazing and, playing his flute, approached Argus.

The giant was fascinated by the sweet melody and begged Hermes to stop there with him, never imagining that the god wanted just to remain there. Argus listened, fascinated by the sweet sound, but he did not yield to sleep; he even asked who had invented that melodious instrument. The god then began to tell the story of Pan and

Syrinx, of the unrequited love of Pan, who created from the reeds of the marsh, the musical instrument that he called "syringe" in honor of the girl he loved. Gradually, lulled by the sweet sound of the flute and the words of Hermes, the giant closed all one hundred eyes.

Once Argus was asleep Hermes killed him by cutting off his head with the sword, and he freed Io from captivity. With the killing of Argus, the spell had been broken, and in place of the heifer, there was now the same beautiful girl as before.

Hermes then carried her to his kingdom, while Hera, irritated, became aware of the death of the guardian. Then she thought to take the one hundred eyes of Argus and with them, decorate the tail of the peacock, which was an animal sacred to her. Then she stared at the stars in the firmament that still form the constellation of the Peacock, an eternal reminder of Argus.

Another version of the legend says that Io did not turn immediately into the girl, but while still a heifer, had to suffer other abuses by Hera. In fact, the goddess sent a gadfly to torment poor Io.To escape it, she jumped into the sea and swam a great distance across the sea that now bears her name and has become known as the Ionian Sea.

Then she crossed other seas in Europe and Asia, and eventually she landed in Egypt. Here, finally, she resumed human form and became the mother of Epaphus, son of Zeus. Hera still tried to hurt her, having the Curetes kidnap her son, but after many adventures, Io finally found him and lived with him in the land of Egypt.

Analysis and Understanding

1) Who was Argus and what does the name "Panoptes" mean?
2) Which deeds did he perform?
3) Argus is the protagonist of what story?
4) Who was Io?
5) To what animal was Io transformed by Zeus?
6) Whom did goddess Hera call as the guardian?
7) What did Zeus do then?
8) Which god did he send to rescue her?
9) What did the goddess Hera do with the eyes of Argus?
10) Which constellation did she stare at in the sky?

Reworking and Writing

1) Imagine the conversation between the god Hermes disguised as a shepherd and the giant Argus and transcribe it in your notebook.

2) The Aegean Sea is named for a character of a legend; can you tell who he was and in what myth we find him?

3) Do a search on the names of seas around Italy, seeking the etymology.

3) Even today they say "having the eyes of Argus": explain in your own words what this saying means.

The Erinyes

The ancient Greeks also believed in the Erinyes (who were later called Furies in Roman mythology), goddesses of vengeance, represented as monstrous winged female figures. Some say they had bat wings and terrible eyes dripping blood. Sometimes they were represented with bronze feet, entwined snakes in their hair and holding torches, lashes or whips.

Legend has it that they were born from the blood of the god Uranus when he was wounded by Cronus. Another version of the myth says that they were the daughters of Night and lived in Tartarus, the dark underground world; yet another legend says that they were descendants of Earth. Their number was initially variable, then it was fixed at three. Their names were Alecto, "the incessant", Megera, "envious", and Tisifone, "avenging the murder."

They punished the crimes and evil deeds which were not discovered by the human justice. Mostly they lived in Hades, where they administered justice and punished the guilty. Sometimes they left the realm of the Underworld and climbed to Earth, even to persecute the living who were guilty of horrendous crimes. They especially punished those bloody crimes perpetrated against their own race, that is, against relatives, causing the culprit to go insane or provoking other mortals to take revenge on them.

They also punished perjurers, those who did not keep their provided oaths, and even those who disobeyed their parents and elders, who behaved badly against the weakest, who did not respect the laws of hospitality, and who rage against supplicants, i.e., those who were asking for mercy.

In general, their revenge was directed against all those who did not respect the ethical norms and the laws of morality. The Erinyes were thus the guardians of social order, and thus they punished those who disturbed that order.

Also, they prevented the soothsayers from predicting the future too clearly because in men there had to remain a degree of uncertainty about what would happen in the future. They caused an unbearable guilt in their victims, leading them to madness.

A sanctuary at Colonus, a suburb of Athens, was dedicated to them, but they were also venerated in other places in Greece.

Mortals were so afraid to pronounce their names that they were often called by the nickname of "Eumenides", "the benevolent", a name which may also refer to the state of restoring order to the good, after the punishment of the wicked.

It's also likely that the name Eumenides refers to the justice entrusted to city courts after the democratic reform in Athens, which established penalties according to the law, as opposed to the previous private justice that was implemented with blood.

Analysis and Understanding

1) What were the Erinyes called by the Romans?
2) How were they represented?
3) Where were they born, according to various legends?
4) How many were they?
5) What were their names and what did they mean?
6) Where did they live mostly?
7) What crimes did they punish?
8) What did they cause the victims?
9) Where was the most important shrine dedicated to them?
10) How were they also called?

Reworking and Writing

1) In ancient times in Greece, as in other countries, hospitality was considered a sacred duty. Those guilty of crimes against the host were considered responsible for an enormous crime. It was not by chance that they were punished so forcefully by the

Erinyes. Do a search on the duty of hospitality in the ancient world.

2) During the fifth century B.C. Athens went from an oligarchic government, i.e., rule by a few, generally aristocrats, to a democratic government in which the power was given to the people through their representatives ("demos" in Greek means "the people"). With the help of the history book, trace a brief summary of the relevant period at issue.

3) The Erinyes are also described in Dante's Divine Comedy (Inferno, IX, vv. 34-51). Try to paraphrase the following passage:

"...Yet more
He added: but I hold it not in mind,
For that mine eye toward the lofty tower
Had attracted me wholly, to its burning top.
Where in an instant I beheld uprisen
At once three hellish furies stained with blood:
In limb and motion, feminine they seemed;
Around them, greenest hydras twisting rolled
Their volumes; adders and cerastes crept
Instead of hair, and their fierce temples bound.
He knowing well the miserable hags
Who tend the queen of endless woe, thus spake:
"See the fierce Erinyes. To the left
This is Megaera; on the right hand she,
Who wails, Alecto; and Tisiphone
Is in the midst." This said, in silence he remained
Their breast they each one clawing tore; themselves

Smote with their palms, and such shrill clamour
raised,
That to the poet I clung, full of suspicion."

"The myth is the foundation of life,

the timeless pattern,

the formula by which

it is expressed

when it escapes out of

unconsciousness."

Thomas Mann

eBook Kindle:
http://www.amazon.it/dp/B01BRHAM5W

6) "Phoenix – Poesie giovanili"

eBook Kindle:
http://www.amazon.it/dp/B01CDEOZSI

7) "Phoenix ", poesie, Lalli Editore, 1985

8) "Dei, eroi e miti. Le più belle storie della mitologia greca" – edizione cartacea

252 pages

ISBN-13: 978-1530283538 (CreateSpace-Assigned)

ISBN-10: 1530283531

https://www.createspace.com/6104204

9) "Amores. Gli amori degli dei, degli eroi e degli uomini" – edizione cartacea

284 pages

ISBN-13: 978- 1530992072 (CreateSpace-Assigned)

ISBN-10: 1530992072

https://www.createspace.com/6200052

www.ingramcontent.com/pod-product-compliance
Lightning Source LLC
Chambersburg PA
CBHW070910180626
46817CB00003B/998